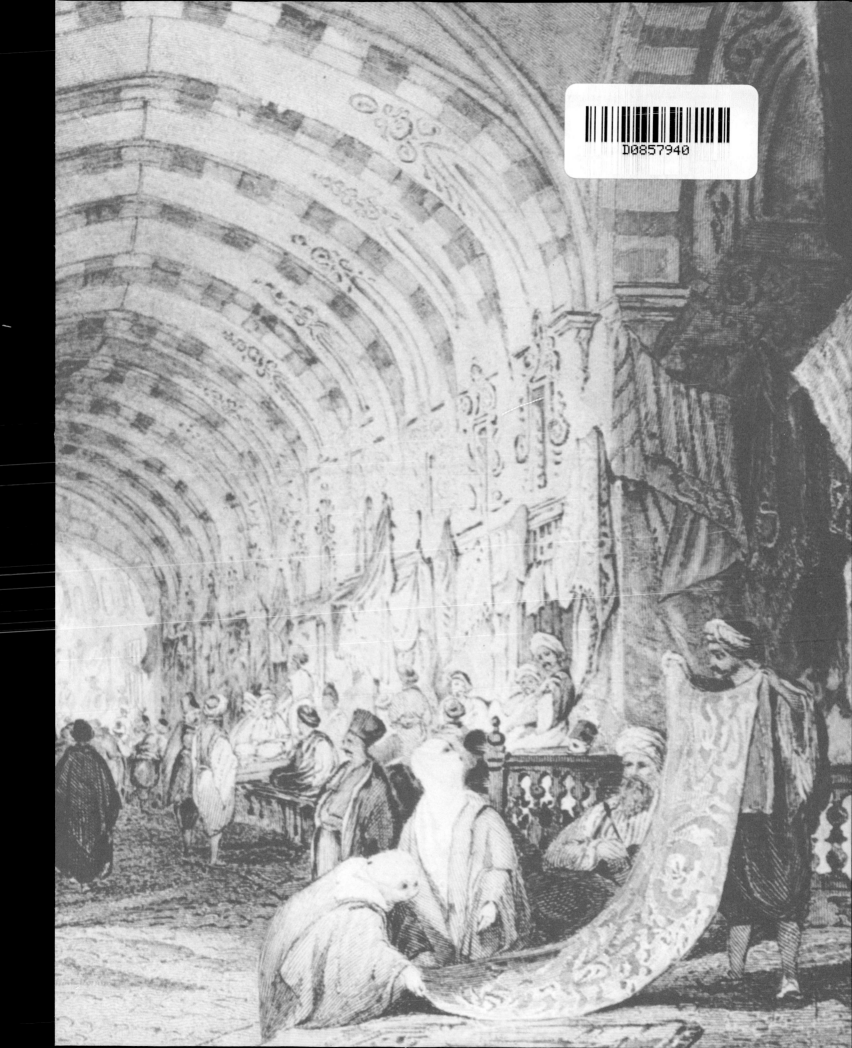

Oriental Rugs

THE SMITHSONIAN ILLUSTRATED LIBRARY OF ANTIQUES

General Editor: Brenda Gilchrist

Oriental Rugs

Walter B. Denny

COOPER-HEWITT MUSEUM

The Smithsonian Institution's National Museum of Design

ENDPAPERS

The Great Bazaar in Istanbul. An illustration by Thomas Allom from Robert Walsh's *Constantinople and the Scenery of the Seven Churches of Asia Minor*, 1840.

FRONTISPIECE

Among the great number of *sejjadeh* rugs woven in central Anatolia, one occasionally finds a masterpiece such as this. Late nineteenth century. 132 x 109 cm. (4 ft. 4 in. x 3 ft. 7 in.). Private collection

Art Direction, Design: JOSEPH B. DEL VALLE

Text Editor: JOAN HOFFMAN

Picture Editor: LISA LITTLE

Contents

Introduction

A rug is a heavy textile used for a variety of utilitarian purposes in the form in which it left the loom. In other words, unlike other kinds of textiles, rugs are meant to be used intact, or sewn together with other rugs, but are only rarely cut or tailored in any way. In rug-producing societies, we find rugs employed in many practical and symbolic tasks, from covering floors to decorating camels. For those of us accustomed to applying the term *rug* exclusively to floor covering, this very broad definition may come as a surprise. But as the following pages will show, any other definition is unduly limiting. The term *carpet* in this book refers to a rug of some size whose primary use is to cover a flat surface, whether a wall, floor or tabletop; and for our purposes a carpet is a specialized type of rug.

Aside from being uncommonly difficult to define, rugs have additional characteristics which set them apart from other categories in the decorative arts. For one thing, rugs have been produced in and for all strata of society, from the wealthiest nobility to the humblest peasantry. Historically, only a small proportion of all woven rugs were intended as items of trade; most were intended to be used in the very place where they were created, the village house or the nomadic tent, or by the very person for whom they were woven on special commission. To study rugs is not only to study the range and beauty of a series of quite amazing artistic objects—it is also to study a way of life, now fast disappearing, in which for untold centuries all aspects of visual expression were given form through the medium of weaving. For in that society where the woven rug originated, the entire cycle of human existence was closely linked to the textiles forming its economic and cultural lifeblood. Children were cradled in hammocks made from rugs; clothes and food were stored and transported in bags made of rugs; a young woman's eligibility for marriage was predicated in large part on her ability to weave beautifully, and her wedding ceremony was held amidst specially woven rug decorations.

Colorplate 1.
From the Sehna district of Iranian Kurdistan, this tiny rug, with its compact knotting and single wefts drawn tightly between rows of knots, shows the skillful adaptation of a design usually found in larger rugs to a small format only rarely encountered in the district. Early twentieth century. 81 x 67 cm. (2 ft. 8 in. x 2 ft. 2 in.). George Walter Vincent Smith Art Museum, Springfield, Mass.

The very identity of the tribal group which constituted the basic social unit was expressed by the designs of its woven rugs.

From these origins, the medium of the woven rug and its stylistic attributes changed as the art form reached into different social and economic areas of traditional society. At some early time, as the making of rugs moved from nomadic encampments to villages and towns, rugmaking became a commercial enterprise, and carpets which traveled far and wide on the highways of commerce served as vehicles for the exchange of artistic ideas and styles among weaving centers throughout the rugmaking world. And when royal carpet manufactories were established at the courts of reigning monarchs, the medium of the woven rug was subjugated by the elegant rhythms and complex artistry of the professional court artist, whose trade was plied with pen on paper and whose sense of color was developed in the rarefied and brilliant world of illuminated and illustrated manuscripts. Remote from the highland meadows and village hearths where the medium originated as part of a fundamental way of life, the art of the rug was elevated to an extraordinary artistic achievement, the one-of-a-kind creations destined for the palaces of great rulers.

In time, the techniques and to a great extent the designs of woven rugs began to radiate outward from those cultures where rug weaving had formed an integral part of common, commercial and court patterns of living. Today, in an age dominated by the mechanized production of all life's necessities, the traditional, or "oriental," rug, woven in the Islamic Near and Middle East, in China and in their cultural provinces, is one of the few art forms still produced by hand in age-old patterns and techniques relatively untouched by the technological changes of the past century and a half. But in a very short time the art of handweaving rugs will have died, and soon thereafter the technique itself will disappear. This book must of necessity spend much time looking backward, for it is written in the twilight of the handwoven rug, as foreign values and the relentless pressures of economic survival in the twentieth century bring an end to an art and a way of life.

1 Techniques of Rug Weaving

Many rug scholars are fond of talking about a "rug belt" in which the majority of the world's rugs have been produced. North of the rug belt, it is too cold for the production of the basic fibers and dyestuffs which go into the making of rugs, while to the south, according to the accepted rule, the weather is too hot for heavy textiles, and artistic energies are channeled into other mediums. As a matter of fact, there is much truth in this definition of the geographical homeland of rug weaving (map 1, see page 10). Rugs were woven in Spain; they are still woven in the Maghrib, the northwestern corner of Africa. In former times rugs were woven in Egypt, and in Syria to the north. Rugs are woven today in Asia Minor (Asiatic Turkey) and were once woven in great numbers in the Balkan provinces of the Ottoman Empire. To the east, rugs formed a basic element of the artistic expression in that complex ethnic and geographical grab bag we call the Caucasus. In the land of Iran, from its northern frontiers on the Caucasus and Central Asia to its southern province of Fars, rugs have been woven for many centuries. Northward and eastward, in the steppes and deserts of Central Asia, all the way to the bleak wastes of Mongolia and southward into China and India, rug weaving has long been established as a traditional art.

This, then, is the traditional rug belt. It was distinguished until recently by an abundance of the essential ingredients of a rug: an ample supply of fiber, in most cases wool; a social order in which handicrafts were encouraged and made up a basic element of the socialization process for young persons, especially young women; and finally, and perhaps most important, cheap labor.

In modern times, the importance of the last of these three factors has eclipsed that of the others. Wool can be easily and quickly shipped to all parts of the world; the modern era has changed, and in many cases destroyed, the values which encouraged the arduous, time-consuming and patient arts of the human hand; and the weaving of rugs,

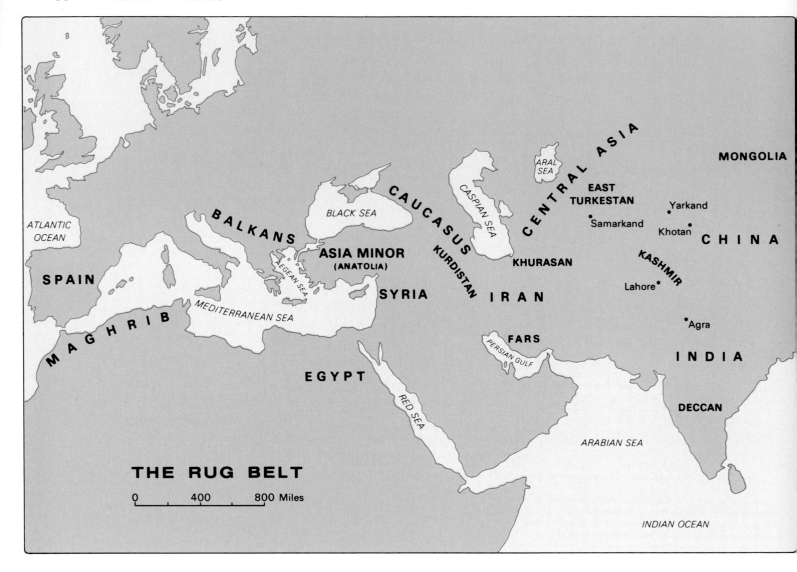

wrenched stem and root from its original soil, is now accomplished
more and more on a commercial level in factories located where cheap
labor allows the most economical production. The art of rug weaving
as folk art or fine art is dying, but commercial production continues
and now takes place in many areas outside the traditional geographical
homeland of the rug.

A further look at our map will confirm yet another factor common
to most of the traditional rug belt. The majority of the countries in
this area are, or were at some important part of their history, countries
where the predominant religion and cultural orientation is Islam, a
religion and a way of life founded in the seventh century of our era
by the Arab prophet Muhammad. The weaving of rugs appears to be

deeply rooted in the ancient tribal life of Central Asian nomadic peoples; as these peoples converted to the Islamic religion and adopted Islamic customs, they in turn impressed upon the culture of Islam the important role played by the woven rug in their society. In Islamic society woven rugs became synonymous with wealth, and their decorations incorporated the symbology of religious, royal and mystical ideologies. Just as techniques of weaving spread out from humble villages and encampments to influence the artistic creations of the Islamic courts, so the rarefied symbolism of the Islamic court gradually moved, with its accompanying visual forms, into village and nomadic weaving. At the same time, the folk symbols and tribal lore of the distant, even pre-Islamic, past continued as powerful undercurrents in the weaving of villages and encampments.

The process of rugmaking starts with the basic physical ingredient of a textile: fiber. In most traditional rug-weaving societies, the fiber most frequently used was the wool of the sheep (plate 1), which was found in abundance in nomadic and village societies. Wool even in our synthetic age is the most miraculous of fibers. While wool on the surface of a sheep may look somewhat undisciplined and carry a distinctly repellent olfactory message, wool on the surface of a rug—reactive to light and gleaming in a multitude of beautiful colors—provides a delightful experience for the senses of sight and touch. Properly treated, wool not only holds its colors better than many other fibers but is uncommonly resistant to wear, rot, mildew and other lurking enemies of woven textiles.

A suitable number of sheep having been caught and rendered more or less immobile, the wool is liberated from its original hosts by means of iron or steel hand-shears (plate 2). The fleece, off-white, dirty, verminous, matted, oily and with an unspeakable fragrance, must then be cleaned. A simple soap and the running water of a stream or spring, catalyzed by the application of tremendous physical force in the form of a mattock, which beats the wet, soapy fleece against a flat rock, combine to render the by now hopelessly matted fleece more or less clean but looking less than ever like our conception of a woven rug.

The next step in the preparation of wool for weaving is to apply to the clean but matted fibers a comblike instrument, called a *carding comb*, that takes different forms in different rug-weaving areas. Bit by bit, the clean matted wool is changed into a fluffy white mass of loosely packed fibers which lie more or less parallel. These fibers are then converted into yarn by the process known as spinning.

The tool for accomplishing this purpose, known as a *spindle*, is made of wood and in many ways resembles an old-fashioned top, although much longer and thinner (plate 3). As the first step in the spinning process, from a fluffy handful of carded wool a small portion of fiber is pulled, twisted and attached to the head of the spindle.

1.

The scientific breeding of sheep for wool is a comparatively recent phenomenon in the Near East. The offspring of this splendid ram will carry genes for improved fleece to many villages in Turkey. Outskirts of İstanbul, 1972

2.

Removing the oily, matted fleece from the sheep is the first step in the making of a rug in the Near Eastern village. Today electric clippers are beginning to replace the traditional locally forged hand-shears. Hazar Lake, near Elazigh, Turkey, 1973

3.

The spinner and her spindle. Slowly, centimeter by centimeter, the woolen yarns which will form the warp, weft and pile of the rug are spun and then, if necessary, plied together before dyeing. Lâdik, Turkey, 1973

Next, while the left hand holds the carded wool, the spindle is twirled against the right thigh with the right hand and then dropped, twisting the yarn and slowly pulling it out of the mass of carded wool. If the spinner slaps at the spindle upward on the thigh, a counterclockwise spin, known as a *Z-spin*, results; while if the direction of the spinning hand is downward on the thigh, a clockwise or *S-spin* is obtained (figure 1). After a meter or more of yarn has been spun, the newly made yarn is stored by winding it around the top of the spindle, more wool is added to the fluffy mass held in the left hand and the process is repeated. Meter after meter of yarn may be drawn from the left hand, spun and wound around the spindle until the spindle becomes too heavy to spin with ease.

Woolen yarn so spun can then be *plied* (twisted) into thicker yarns by pulling spun yarn out of two or more balls and using the spindle to ply two or more strands together. The plying is usually the reverse of the spinning; therefore, Z-spun yarns are generally plied together clockwise, producing an S-ply yarn. Thus, arduously, hundreds of meters of yarn, the basic material of the woven rug, are accumulated.

On occasion, depending on the local supply, other fibers were used by rug weavers, and of these cotton was the most common. While not possessing wool's strength, reactivity to light and ability to create marvelous effects with color, cotton is a considerably more tractable fiber, and rugs woven with cotton structural material, i.e., *warps* and *wefts*, are not only easier to make in purely physical terms but also tend to lie flatter once completed. Sometimes other fibers, such as goat hair, camel hair or silk, were employed in rug weaving either as *foundation* (warp and weft) or as the *knotted pile*. Silk, of all natural fibers the most reactive to light and the most delightful to touch, was also the most expensive, the most prone to wear and the least likely to retain its color over time, and we expect to see silk used primarily in rugs destined to be admired but not put to hard physical use. Silk could also be woven into extremely fine yarns, and was often used as warp and weft in rugs of fine weave with silk or wool pile.

Once the yarns are spun and plied, they are dyed when their use demands some color other than the ivory off-white of undyed wool. The dyeing process is the most technologically complex stage in the creation of the rug, involving chemical processes which in former times were not fully understood even by their most experienced practitioners. The traditional wool dyer was a sort of alchemist, turning basic woolen yarns, by means of simple herbs, roots and powders, into glorious colored yarns reflecting a multitude of hues. From the root of the madder plant the dyer extracted a wonderful red whose hue could be varied according to the amount of time the yarn spent in the boiling dye pot, the type of spring water used and the amount

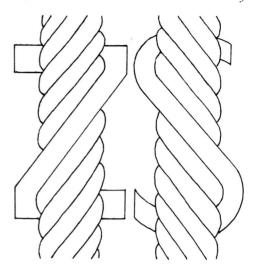

Figure 1.
Yarn spun or plied in a counterclockwise direction follows the diagonal of a Z (*left*); clockwise, an S.

and type of *mordant* used. The latter was a chemical which rendered the wool susceptible to absorption of the dyestuffs, and in traditional rug-weaving areas mordants included such varied materials as yoghurt and alum. In addition to the several reds derived from madder, a purplish red, which was more temperamental and prone to bleed, was created from a lac-type insect extract called cochineal. Blue was produced from indigo, and yellow from various flower petals. These basic hues could be mixed to provide green, violet and orange; more exotic hues were made from other plant, animal and mineral materials. The yarn was dyed skein by skein, and the dyes themselves were frequently produced in the time-honored tradition of "a pinch of this and a handful of that"; the result quite naturally was that one skein of wool was not quite the same color as the next, and the concept of a large, uniform dye-lot was totally lacking. Consequently, in the finished rug there were often subtle variations in color over the woven fabric which much enhanced the visual interest of the rug. This phenomenon, known as *abrash*, is an aesthetic by-product of a simple technological process, which, if not unduly obtrusive, greatly contributes to the charm and loveliness of traditional rugs, but which is all but lost in our own time.

After the dyeing, the wool is washed to remove excess dye, and the skeins of dyed yarn are hung out in the sun to dry. It is at this point that the preparation of the yarns ends, and the actual process of weaving begins, starting with the preparation of the loom.

A simple village or nomadic loom, more complex versions of which still retain its basic elements, is little more than a large rectangular frame of heavy wooden construction, which can either be laid flat,

4.
The flat loom is favored by nomadic and seminomadic peoples because of its simplicity and because it can be dismantled easily. The one being set up here has part of the warp in place. Van, Turkey, 1973

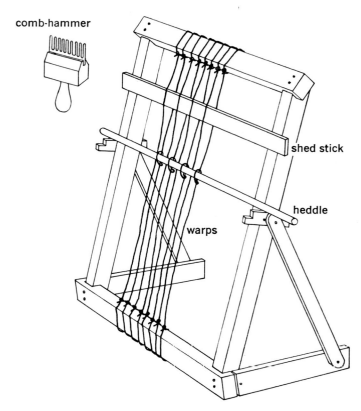

comb-hammer

shed stick

heddle

warps

Figure 2.
Vertical loom.

propped up on a few bricks or stones (plate 4) or by the addition of a base and bracing made into a vertical loom (figure 2). On this simple frame is stretched a warp of undyed fiber, usually wool in village or nomadic rugs and cotton or silk in commercial or court rugs. With the entire warp, or longitudinal part of the foundation of the woven rug, in place, the loom resembles a sort of rectangular harp with many parallel strings. Depending on the type of loom and upon local weaving traditions, these "strings" may either be crowded close together, producing a rug with a very strong and closely packed structure, or they may be separated from each other by the width of a fraction of a centimeter.

Weaving, as most of us are familiar with it, is composed of two basic elements. One is the warp, which forms the basis upon which the other elements of a woven fabric are in fact woven. The other basic component of weaving is the weft, the latitudinal strand which turns a set of parallel warp strands into a true fabric. The weft yarns are put into place by weaving them continuously over and under the warp threads across the width of the rug. This is accomplished by means of two very simple devices, the *shed stick* and the *heddle* (figure 2). The shed stick is usually a flat stick which is inserted through the warps, separating them so that alternate warp threads are above and below the shed stick. When the slatlike stick is turned on its side, the sets of warps can be separated by sufficient space (the *shed*)

Figure 3.
Slit-tapestry weave.

Colorplate 2.
The finely woven *kilim* rugs of the Sehna district of Iranian Kurdistan show intricate designs which have overcome the usual limitations of the *kilim's* slit-tapestry technique. Few Sehna *kilims*, however, have the fresh colors and soft, pliable wool of this remarkable example. Late nineteenth century. 183 x 137 cm. (6 ft. x 4 ft. 6 in.). Detail. George Walter Vincent Smith Art Museum, Springfield, Mass.

to pass, or *shoot*, the weft between them across the width of the rug. In order to pass the weft back across the rug so that it now passes below those warps it formerly passed above, and above those it formerly passed below, the heddle is used. The heddle is a stick, laid above the warps across the width of the loom, from which a strong woolen or cotton string is first passed *under* one of the warps relegated to the *lower* level by the shed stick; the string then passes back *over* the heddle stick and loops below the next of the lower warps, until a series of loops has captured each of the lower warp threads across the width of the loom. When the shed stick is laid flat, and a healthy pull is exercised on the heddle stick, those warps which were formerly lower on the loom are pulled through the upper warps to a higher level. The weft yarn may then be passed back across the loom, now passing over those warps it had passed under on its original journey, and under those warps it had passed over. Repetition of this process produces the most common form of woven fabric, appropriately named *plain weave*.

If this weft yarn happens to be colored, and the warp thread is undyed, the result is a "salt-and-pepper" surface speckled with white warp. But if the weft is passed across the loom fairly loosely, it can be packed down on the warp with the so-called comb-hammer, a curious tool which looks like a cross between a hammer and a comb (figure 2), thereby completely hiding the warps (colorplate 2).

One result of this is the weaving category known as the *weft-faced tapestry weave*, and we find that some of the simplest rugs are woven in precisely this technique. Designs of horizontal bands can be created by changing the color of the weft at particular intervals, but the technique limits the weaver to simple horizontal stripe designs.

More complex designs can be created by the use of the *slit-tapestry* technique, a variety of the weft-faced tapestry weave, in which areas of different colors meeting along the warps leave slits in the rug fabric (figure 3 and colorplate 2). More commonly known in the Near East as *kilim* weaving, this slit-tapestry technique is used from China to central Europe. Employing very fine warps and wefts allows for the creation of designs of quite astonishing fluidity and complexity in *kilim* weave (colorplate 2), but the technique generally influences the design in the direction of simple, geometrical forms (colorplate 10, see page 56). Another characteristic of slit-tapestry rugs is that long vertical straight lines in the design are impossible, and various accommodations in design and technique evolved as a result. In some tapestry weaving, most notably that of southern Iran, this problem was overcome by interlocking wefts of different colors around a shared warp.

Tapestry-woven examples are among the simplest of the so-called *flat-woven rugs*, which were produced largely in village and nomadic societies. Another kind of flat-woven rug is the *brocaded rug*, in

Figure 4.
Sumak brocading.

which the design is added to the plain-weave foundation by means of *supplementary wefts*. Brocaded rugs take many forms, but among the most prevalent is the *sumak* (plate 59, see page 86), where the extra wefts from which the design is formed are wrapped over four warps, back under two and over four and so forth (figure 4). Other types of brocading are much simpler, but all involve weaving in the design wefts at the same time that the plain-weave foundation is woven on the loom. When decoration is put in afterward, with a needle, it is known as *embroidery*; in traditional rug-weaving societies, brocading was preferred to embroidery for most rug-type textiles.

But the kind of rug most of us think of when we hear the term rug is the kind technically known as the *pile rug*. Pile rugs are made of row after row of tiny knots tied on the warps of the foundation, which by the thousands combine to create a thick, fuzzy, light-reactive fabric. Pile rugs may be woven in a variety of knot types traditional to particular rug-weaving areas and peoples. The best-known knots (figure 5) are the *symmetrical*, or *Turkish*, knot (sometimes called the *Gördes knot* after the rug center in western Turkey) and the two forms of the *asymmetrical*, or *Persian*, knot (often called the *Sehna knot* after the Persian weaving area of Sanandaj, or Sehna). In fact, there is no specific geographical homeland of either the Turkish or the Persian knot, and both are used all over the Muslim world.

To make a knotted-pile rug, the weaver starts at one side of the rug and ties a knot on the first two warps. Moving across the rug, the weaver continues along, using various colored yarns as required by the pattern and tying knot after knot on successive pairs of warps (plate 5). Once a row of knots has been completed across the rug, the shed stick and heddle are manipulated and weft is shot across the rug, from one to as many as eight times. The weft is then beaten with a comb-hammer to make the fabric solid and compact. Following this, the weaver ties the next row of knots. As soon as a considerable area is knotted, the rug is trimmed with special scissors to the desired pile length, and the design emerges, composed of small "dots" of colored yarns which form the pile. Clearly the pile rug takes a large amount of wool and labor, and for its many aesthetic and practical advantages commands a high price. It is in the medium of the pile rug that the great traditions of rug weaving have produced perhaps their best-known offspring, but we should remember that the technique is but one of many used in traditional rug-weaving societies.

Other aspects vital to our knowledge of rugs emerge from our understanding of the technique of weaving. One of the most characteristic aspects lies in the construction of edges and ends; although designs, colors and fibers were frequently borrowed, the edge and end finishes of rugs tended to follow strict local traditions. The *selvedge* (edge) of a rug may be of different colors; it may be round and thick like a cable, or wide and flat, and it may be striped

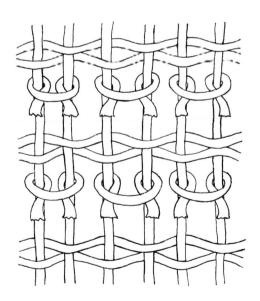
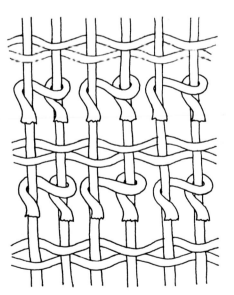
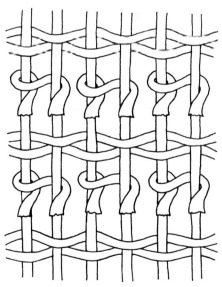

Figure 5.
Rug knots (*left to right*): symmetrical (Turkish or Gördes); asymmetrical (Persian or Sehna), open on the left; asymmetrical (Persian or Sehna), open on the right.

5.
The weaver pulls out two warps at a time in order to tie the knots in colored yarns which, when trimmed to even length, will form the pile of the completed carpet. Kayseri, Turkey, 1973

or of one color. The ends of the rug may sport long fringes or complicated patterns of knots. Some rugs may employ a broad band, or *skirt*, of tapestry weave at each end (plate 62, see page 96); others may include stripes of flat-woven brocaded decoration. Although edges and ends are the first parts of a rug to be damaged through wear, and are often restored or replaced, when the original edge and end finishes are left intact they tell a great deal about a rug's origins and age.

Another important aspect of a rug is its surface reactivity to light. Some rugs, designed for floor use, may use a strong, "hard" wool in a finely knotted and very short pile. Such rugs may be woven with ease in complex and curvilinear patterns, but they do not "shine" in a strong light. Other rugs, with longer pile, and using softer wool much less resistant to wear, may react to light in a more vivacious manner. When the weaver ties her knots, she pulls them downward in place, and the degree to which the pile "leans" may also affect the rug's tendency to shine. All rugs have a "right" direction for stroking, like the back of a cat, and the pile always leans toward the end at which the weaving of the rug began.

One last aspect of a rug stemming directly from its technique is its feel; some rugs, of very heavy construction, may be as stiff and as heavy as plywood, while others, of lighter construction, may be as flexible and as supple as a handkerchief. The feel of a rug may sometimes tell us more about a rug's origins than any visual aspect of its design or construction; a connoisseur of carpets can often make an accurate attribution blindfolded.

One other form of rug which should be mentioned here—seldom exported to the West, and lowest in status of the family of rugs—is the *felt rug*. Felt rugs are known to have been made from very ancient times (plate 6) and are still produced today all over the Islamic world. A felt rug is a nonwoven rug made directly from carded wool, in the process known as *fulling*, by sprinkling the wool with a mixture of very hot water and alkaline soap and then repeatedly pressing or "treading" it into a compact slab. Designs are often formed by adding unspun dyed carded wool in patterns to the surface of the slab before the final steaming and pressing process. Felt rugs are not particularly prized for their aesthetic merits or their strength, but felt's adaptability to stretching and molding and its excellent insulating qualities have led it to be used in the making of saddle covers, boots and shepherds' cloaks, as well as those tentlike structures known as yurts, in areas of extreme cold.

There was a time when the collector of rugs paid very little attention to the complexities of technique, and our knowledge of the technical characteristics of various rug types was rather minimal. The serious student of rugs now realizes the immense importance of understanding the process of creating a rug. Rug scholars today employ various forms of notation in describing the technique of a rug; a typical technical analysis notes the material, color, ply and direction of spin and twist of warp, weft and pile yarns, together with the density of knotting and the characteristics of the pile, edges and ends. While technical analyses in and of themselves can be quite baffling or boring to the lay person, a basic knowledge of technique contributes vastly not only to the intellectual appreciation of rugs but to the enjoyment of rugs as well.

6.
By stitching strips of thin felt to a piece of thicker felt, the creator of this handsome multicolored felt rug, which was made to be used as a saddle cover, has depicted a griffin attacking a mountain goat. The extraordinary artifact was excavated in Barrow 1 at Pazyryk in Siberia. Fifth century B.C. Dimensions not given. Detail. State Hermitage Museum, Leningrad

2 The Historical Development of Rugs

The history of the rug as an art form is long and complicated, and many crucial aspects are still the cause of lively scholarly debate. In a general introduction, naturally only the broadest outlines of the historical development can be sketched in, and the writer who departs from the crooked and narrow path of consensus is treading dangerous ground indeed. Until quite recently, the oldest rugs known to us in the knotted-pile technique were Islamic carpets dating to about the thirteenth or fourteenth century, and while historical sources mention earlier rugs in the Islamic tradition, no examples seem to have survived. In any event, the entire historical perspective on rugs was suddenly and dramatically changed with the discovery in the late 1940s, in the famous frozen tombs of the Scythians in the Pazyryk Valley of the Altai Mountains of Siberia, of a group of rugs still encased in the solid ice in which they had been preserved since the fifth century B.C. Several felt rugs were excavated (plate 6), but the most interesting fabric found in the Pazyryk tombs was a knotted-pile rug woven in the symmetrical knot which predated the oldest pile rug then known to us by almost seventeen hundred years (plate 7). The design, a tilelike central field with two main borders, one showing horses with riders and grooms, the other fallow deer, has been linked variously with the traditions of the Achaemenian Persian empire to the south and with the art of the nomadic Scythian warriors themselves. Whatever the source of the design, the Pazyryk Carpet represents both an assurance of the pile-woven rug's tradition of extreme venerability and an embarrassment to scholars, who are faced with the chasm of the years between 500 B.C. and A.D. 1200.

Those earliest surviving Islamic carpets noted previously were found at the beginning of this century in mosques in the Turkish towns of Konya and Beyshehir. Comprising more than two dozen complete rugs or fragments (plate 8), the carpets were at first lauded as the survivors of the rugs seen by Marco Polo when he passed

Colorplate 3.
The octagonal medallions of the Turkish large-patterned Holbein are among the earliest-known Islamic carpet patterns, and their influence may be seen in contemporary and later carpets woven in places as diverse as Spain and the Caucasus. Early sixteenth century. 430 x 200 cm. (14 ft. x 6 ft. 7 in.). Detail. Museum für Islamische Kunst, Staatliche Museen, Preussischer Kulturbesitz, West Berlin

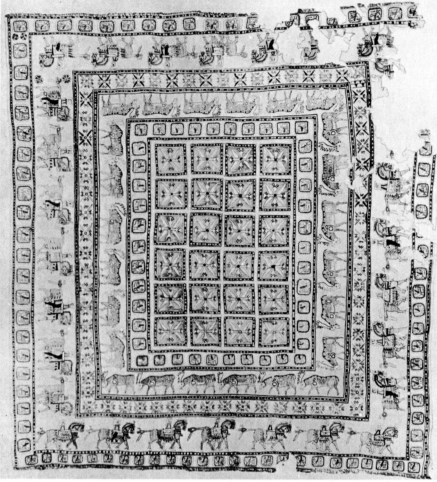

7   8

7.
Discovered in Barrow 5 at the Pazyryk excavations in Siberia, and datable to the fifth century B.C., the Pazyryk Carpet is the oldest-known example of knotted-pile weaving in the world. 200 x 189 cm. (6 ft. 7 in. x 6 ft. 2 in.). State Hermitage Museum, Leningrad

8.
The complete rugs and fragments found in Turkey in the Great Mosque of Konya and the mosque at Beyshehir are the earliest surviving Islamic carpets. This fragment shows a rather simple inter-laced lattice on a dark blue ground, with an equally unsophisticated border design. Thirteenth or fourteenth century. Size of fragment: 320 x 240 cm. (10 ft. 6 in. x 7 ft. 11 in.). Detail, ripped and torn. Museum of Turkish and Islamic Art, İstanbul

through Anatolia in the thirteenth century, and which he praised as the most beautiful carpets in all the world. A hard look at them, however, convinced many scholars that although of undoubted age the rugs found in Konya and Beyshehir were in all probability common commercial carpets of large size, with rather unskillful designs, unlikely to impress a sophisticated thirteenth-century Venetian like Marco Polo. Although attempts to relate their designs to thirteenth- or fourteenth-century stone carving, and to depictions of carpets in fourteenth-century European painting, have proven inconclusive, a conservative assessment of these large, somewhat rough-hewn weavings nevertheless places them in the thirteenth or fourteenth century, and hence they remain, for the time being, the oldest Islamic carpets of which we have knowledge and the second oldest examples of pile-woven carpets known.

In attempting to identify fifteenth-century carpets, we have considerably more luck. By the fifteenth century, under the Ottoman sultans who were to rule Turkey for another five hundred years, carpets were being exported from Asia Minor to Europe in significant numbers and began to be depicted before the altars of churches and in the interiors and on the balconies of upper-class homes in European paintings as well as under the feet of the Virgin in many an altarpiece. These European depictions enable us to verify a few early carpets as fifteenth-century products—for example, the Marby Rug (plate 9) can be placed with assurance in the fifteenth century because of its similarity to rugs in datable fifteenth-century paintings.

The commerce in carpets between East and West seems to have increased dramatically in the sixteenth century, and carpets appear in great profusion in the works of European artists whose names have been lent more or less permanently to the carpets they pictured. Thus, from a major center in western Anatolia, possibly the town of Ushak, come two kinds of Holbein carpets and one design known today as a Lotto carpet. The Holbein rugs seem to have first been made in the fifteenth century; one type, known as a small-patterned Holbein, has a repeating design of small medallions, each defined by a continuous strapwork band (plate 10). The other type, called a large-patterned Holbein, contains a large octagonal medallion, in some examples

9.
The Marby Rug, found in a provincial Swedish village church, is one of the few examples of fifteenth-century Turkish weaving to have survived. The design, of two stylized birds flanking a tree, has ancient origins stretching back to pre-Islamic Central Asia. Fifteenth century. 170 x 112 cm. (5 ft. 7 in. x 3 ft. 8 in.). Skirts partially shown. Statens Historiska Museum, Stockholm

10.

The small interlaced medallions on this early Anatolian rug, a small-patterned Holbein, bespeak a link between commercial production in fifteenth- and sixteenth-century Anatolia and the nomadic weaving tradition of much earlier times in which the medallionlike *gul* form was common. Early sixteenth century. 209 x 140 cm. (6 ft. 10 in. x 4 ft. 7 in.). Textile Museum, Washington, D.C.

11.

The bold pattern of a yellow lattice on a bright red ground is characteristic of the Lotto carpets of western Anatolia. About 1600. 792 x 257 cm. (26 ft. x 8 ft. 5 in.). Detail. Textile Museum, Washington, D.C.

12.

The rarity of oriental carpets, and especially the aura of sanctity attached to them, contributed to their use in the churches of medieval Europe. In this painting, *The Mass of St. Giles*, which dates from about 1500, the unidentified painter known as the Master of St. Giles has accurately depicted a large-patterned Holbein. National Gallery, London

spaced by two smaller octagons, in repeat along the length of the carpet (colorplate 3). The interstices are filled in with many smaller geometric forms. As in the small-patterned Holbeins and many other early Turkish carpets, the borders of the large-patterned Holbeins often feature an interlacing strapwork design which probably originated in architectural decoration and which is derived from a rectilinear form of the Arabic script known as Kufic. The same border is often seen around the Lotto carpets, whose central design is a geometrical stylization of a vegetal lattice which again probably traces its ancestry back to the carved decoration on stone buildings, and whose primary colors will come to typify the brilliant and straightforward "Turkish palette" in carpet weaving for centuries (plate 11).

The popularity of the various types of Turkish carpets continued in the West because of the commercial activities of the Italians, especially the Venetians, who acted as middlemen between European markets and the source of carpets in the Near East. It appears that Turkish carpets were extraordinarily expensive in the sixteenth century, and only the most wealthy Europeans could afford to possess them; we are not surprised, therefore, to see these treasured possessions represented in portraits of European notables. The Church, which since the Middle Ages had used Islamic textiles for ecclesiastical vestments, placed Islamic carpets in a position of great honor in front of the

10

11

altar (plate 12), a tradition still continued in European cathedrals.

It is early in the sixteenth century that the first datable examples of rug weaving appear in Persia, a land whose carpets in our own time have become virtually synonymous with the term oriental rug. While the early rugs of Anatolian Turkey reflect in their geometric designs the four-square nature of the rug-weaving medium, with each knot corresponding to a tiny square in a sheet of graph paper, the earliest-known Persian rugs, thought to have been woven in and around the city of Tabriz in northwestern Iran, had already fallen under the spell of the illuminators and miniaturists of the court library, an institution much beloved of Persian rulers from the fourteenth century onward. More finely woven than their Turkish counterparts, and thus better able to render curvilinear forms through a series of minuscule knots, the early Persian carpets reflect in their designs the arts of manuscript illumination and bookbinding; visual focus in the usually rather long format is provided by a *shamsa*, or medallion (plate 13), symbolic of the divine light with which the Persians believed their heterodox Islamic sect of Shi'ism was endowed. Documentary evidence in the form of Islamic miniature painting, however, indicates that during the sixteenth century a parallel geometric

13

13.
Combining the classical Persian medallion design, elements from carpets depicting the hunt and a wide range of animal motifs rich in symbolic referents, this carpet shows the application of the arts of the illuminated book to pile-woven carpets in Persia. Late sixteenth century. 594 x 300 cm. (19 ft. 6 in. x 10 ft. 6 in.). Detail. Metropolitan Museum of Art, New York, lent by Prince Roman Sanguszko

14.
In the encampment of a wealthy nomadic tribe of the sixteenth century could be found rugs woven both in traditional geometric nomadic style and in the curvilinear pictorial style of the court artists, as seen in this miniature painted about 1540 by Mir Sayyid 'Ali, a well-known artist of the Safavid Persian court. Fogg Art Museum, Cambridge, Mass., gift of John Goelet

17

18

15, 16

15.
One of the renowned pair of Emperor Carpets, so called because Peter the Great supposedly presented them as a gift to the Holy Roman emperor Leopold I, this elegant rug represents the height of Safavid court weaving in the sixteenth century. With their designs of animals amid swirling vines and floral decorative elements, and their rich vermilion ground and dark green border, carpets of this type established the fame of Herat as a Persian weaving center. Mid-sixteenth century. 752 x 330 cm. (24 ft. 8 in. x 10 ft. 10 in.). Detail (half). Metropolitan Museum of Art, New York, Rogers Fund, 1943

16.
Detail of two fighting animals in the field of the Emperor Carpet shown in plate 15.

17.
Keeping the central focus of the medal-

lion carpet and combining it with designs of wild animals from the royal hunt, the smaller medallion carpets of sixteenth-century Persia often represent an adaptation of the designs of the huge carpets made only on royal commission to carpets affordable by lower court officials or suitable as royal gifts. Mid-sixteenth century. 221 x 160 cm. (7 ft. 3 in. x 5 ft. 3 in.). Musée Historique des Tissus, Lyons

18.
Using the Persian device of the central medallion in a form used in Turkey by ceramic artisans from Tabriz as early as the beginning of the fifteenth century, the colorful medallion carpets of Ushak in western Asia Minor are perhaps the most famous products of Turkish looms in the sixteenth century and later. About 1600. 425 x 263 cm. (13 ft. 11 in. x 8 ft. 8 in.). Österreichisches Museum für angewandte Kunst, Vienna

nomadic weaving tradition existed in Persia alongside the elegant curvilinear designs produced in the court workshops (plate 14).

As Persian art, most particularly the art of the illuminated and illustrated manuscript, flowered under the patronage of the Safavid dynasty in the sixteenth century, the designs produced by the court artists radiated outward into the realms of architectural decoration, textiles, metalwork and, above all, carpet weaving. The most celebrated of the great Persian carpets were intended for the holy shrines and luxurious palaces which formed the sacred and secular foci of the Safavid Empire, and their designs, influenced by miniature painting, were often full of the imagery of the hunt (plates 15, 16 and 17), the royal garden, the delights of paradise and the pleasures of wine, all of which were celebrated in contemporary Persian literature.

The institution of the court library spread from Persia eastward into northern India and westward into Turkey, and in the latter part of the sixteenth century Persian court artists themselves emigrated, spreading the Safavid style and blending it with local traditions to the east and west. In Turkey, variations on the Safavid medallion carpets were produced at the weaving center of Ushak, combining the complex Persian designs with the beloved Anatolian primary colors (plate 18). In northern India, the court of the Mughal emperors began to evolve a style of its own in the late sixteenth century, and by the early seventeenth the Persian designs, with their sophisticated discipline of symmetry, were adapted to a much more naturalistic pictorial tradition (colorplate 4). Rugs of the Mughal dynasty, in keeping with their more literal nature, tended to have a "top" and "bottom" (plate 75, see page 108), unlike the Persian carpets, where the principles of symmetry allowed the carpet to be viewed equally well from all directions.

For reasons still obscure, under the second Mamluk dynasty, which ruled Egypt from the fourteenth through the early sixteenth century, a royal carpet manufactory was founded that flourished for a brief time during the late fifteenth and early sixteenth centuries. While in the celebrated Mamluk rugs we may observe some stylistic links to contemporary rug weaving in both Anatolia and northwestern Persia, the Mamluk rugs in general partake of a style, and a color scheme, quite distinct from the styles and color schemes of the rest of the rug-weaving world. The almost iridescent colors, the total absence of white and the different hues in exactly corresponding high saturation produce a complex and visually dazzling surface that in the greatest examples provides perhaps the most purely sensual response obtainable from the world of textiles (colorplate 5).

With the conquest of Mamluk Egypt by the armies of the Ottoman Empire in the year 1517, many of the Mamluk weavers seem to have migrated to the Ottoman capital of İstanbul (known in the West as Constantinople) and the nearby silk-producing center of Bursa. The

Colorplate 4.
This "picture rug" from the Indian subcontinent represents the almost exact reproduction in a pile-woven carpet of a miniature painting complete with bizarrely decorated border. Realistic scenes from the hunt are intermingled with the doings of mythological beasts. First half of the seventeenth century. 243 x 155 cm. (8 ft. x 5 ft. 1 in.). Museum of Fine Arts, Boston, gift of Mrs. F. L. Ames in memory of Frederick L. Ames

19

19.
This example of an Ottoman prayer rug is the most beautiful of the small group of royal prayer rugs woven in the special manufactories at Bursa and Istanbul under direct court control. Its design was drawn first on a paper cartoon by a court artist and then woven into the knotted-pile carpet. Late sixteenth century. 183 x 117 cm. (6 ft. x 3 ft. 10 in.). Österreichisches Museum für angewandte Kunst, Vienna

20.
The Ottoman court carpets were created on looms in the city of Bursa and in İstanbul itself after designs made by professional artists working in the royal library in İstanbul. Their subdued coloration and fluid, calligraphic designs bespeak their origins in the art of the penman. Early seventeenth century. 516 x 292 cm. (16 ft. 11 in. x 9 ft. 7 in.). Detail. Metropolitan Museum of Art, New York, James F. Ballard Collection, gift of James F. Ballard, 1922

Colorplate 5.
Noteworthy for its marvelous state of preservation, which makes clear the important contribution of the lustrous pile wool to the overall visual effect of the Mamluk carpets of Egypt, this example presents a ravishing interplay of blue, red and green hues in virtually the same intensity. Early sixteenth century. 269 x 279 cm. (8 ft. 10 in. x 9 ft. 2 in.). Museum of Fine Arts, Boston

20

21

21.
An example of seventeenth-century central Persian weaving, this fragmentary vase carpet contains the palmette forms that are stylized representations of lotus blossoms. The diagonal floral forms and the background lattice of vines are characteristic of this group of weavings, whether or not the vase design itself is present. Seventeenth century. 366 x 218 cm. (12 ft. x 7 ft. 2 in.). Cut and joined. Metropolitan Museum of Art, New York, James F. Ballard Collection, gift of James F. Ballard, 1922

22.
The silk and metallic-thread Polonaise carpets that have survived into our time show little of the vivid colors that must have originally characterized the silken pile. Nevertheless, these large, incredibly luxurious carpets from later Safavid times still reveal the lavishness of the precious materials that went into the best carpets of the classical age in Persia. About 1620. 420 x 183 cm. (13 ft. 9 in. x 6 ft.). Detail. William Rockhill Nelson Gallery of Art, Kansas City, Mo., Nelson Fund

Mamluk color palette and weaving technique eventually combined with new designs which had migrated westward from northwestern Persia, and the resulting synthesis was the Ottoman court carpet. A very sophisticated type of rug, designed by court artists and woven in many different sizes, the court carpet featured curved leaves and complex imaginary flowers as an important part of its design (plates 19 and 20). These elegant and subtle rhythms were to leave an impression lasting for centuries on Anatolian weaving traditions.

The seventeenth century saw an evolution in the Islamic carpet. In Turkey, the center of Ushak continued to produce carpets with a curious blend of Persian draftsmanship and Turkish coloration,

22

which often took ingenious new forms. In Persia, the precise linear and finely woven techniques of the sixteenth-century court carpets were maintained in the high-grade commercial production of the so-called vase carpets in the south central Persian center of Kerman (plate 21). And in the Persian court a new weaving technique, incorporating loosely woven silk pile in combination with brocaded threads of precious metals, resulted in the production of a type of carpet much broader in its design, in which the texture and glitter of silver, gold and silk were paramount (plate 22). These so-called Polonaise carpets, which were exported to eastern Europe in significant quantities, often as specially made presentation pieces, were only one of many types of carpet produced in Persia under the great Shah 'Abbas I and his successors in the seventeenth century.

In India, the conjunction of inexpensive Indian labor and imported Persian designs, supported by the thriving Indian commerce engaged in by the Portuguese and other European traders, resulted in the production of many large carpets with Persian designs woven in an overall pattern of the stylized lotus blossoms known as palmettes, curved leaves, and the curious wiggly forms derived from Chinese art called cloud bands; such carpets were often found among the furnishings of the wealthy in Europe (plates 24 and 25). Under the Mughal emperors the technique of the knotted-pile carpet was developed to its technical extreme; one celebrated Mughal prayer rug, measuring only the small size of a typical prayer rug, about one by one and a half meters, contains more than four million individually tied woolen knots (colorplate 25, see page 106).

Although the history of the Islamic carpet is written primarily in terms of knotted-pile rugs, we do possess a few classical examples woven in the slit-tapestry technique. The earliest and most famous of these are the silk and metallic-thread *kilims* thought to have been woven in Kashan in central Persia in the late sixteenth and early seventeenth centuries. One example (plate 23) contains in its central cartouche one of the oldest-known carpet motifs, which evidently migrated westward to the Islamic world along with the Mongols in the thirteenth century; it is a design of Chinese origin depicting a dragon in combat with a phoenix, and its appearance in the blue-and-white porcelain avidly sought by Islamic collectors of the fifteenth and sixteenth centuries probably accounts for the particular style of its representation here.

For the collector of more recent oriental rugs, especially those woven in the nineteenth and twentieth centuries, the study of the history of rug weaving is no mere academic exercise. The sixteenth and seventeenth centuries in Islamic weaving in particular constituted a classical age in the truest sense of the term, and the designs and motifs developed then exercised an enormous influence on village, nomadic and commercial rug production in subsequent centuries.

Many of the forms we observe today in simple village rugs, so heavily obscured by the gradual process of stylization as to be almost indecipherable, thus trace their origins back to the court ateliers of Turkey, Persia and India. It is an understanding of this process of stylization that enables us to re-create the chain of stylistic changes through which designs and their meanings have been transmitted from rug to rug over the centuries into our own time as a living art.

23.
One of the rare extant early carpets woven in *kilim*, or slit-tapestry, technique is this example from a group of silk and metallic-thread carpets believed to have been made in Kashan in Persia. Its central medallion shows the Chinese motif of the combat between the dragon and the phoenix in a format taken from the sixteenth-century medallion carpets, which in turn was probably derived directly from Chinese porcelain. Early seventeenth century. 227 x 131 cm. (7 ft. 6 in. x 4 ft. 3 in.). Textile Museum, Washington, D.C.

24.
Well-to-do Dutch families and corpora-
tions treasured the oriental carpets imported in large numbers into prosperous
seventeenth-century Holland, and invariably the rugs occupied important
places whenever their individual or group
portraits were painted. In this group
portrait, *The Regents of the Almoners'
Orphanage, Amsterdam,* by Cornelisz
Troost (1697–1750), great prominence
has been accorded the luxurious carpet
of Persian design covering the table.
Rijksmuseum, Amsterdam

25.
Whatever the changing dictates of fashion and style at the seventeenth-century
French court might decree, nothing could
diminish the prestige and attractiveness
of oriental carpets for the French nobility. Here the painter Philippe de
Champagne (1602–1674) has depicted the
churchman Omer Talon seated next to
a table draped with a seventeenth-century
carpet of Persian design probably woven
in either Herat or northern India. National Gallery of Art, Washington, D.C.,
Samuel H. Kress Collection

3   Turkish Rugs

As we have seen, Turkey, the Islamic land most proximate to the West, was from early times a source of rugs for European collectors. Therefore, when we move to a consideration of those carpets still obtainable by today's collector, we must realize that Turkish nomadic and village rugs have been collected, and highly valued, in the West for a much longer time than the rugs of other rug-weaving lands. Asia Minor, or Anatolia, today's Asiatic Turkey, a land halfway between East and West, has been a bridge of ideas, styles and civilizations for millennia (map 2, see page 44). Once the heartland of the Byzantine Empire, Asia Minor was gradually conquered by the Turks—first the Seljuks and later the Ottomans—from the late eleventh century onward, in time becoming the heartland of the Ottoman Empire, and until comparatively recently presented a polyethnic mix of Greek, Armenian, Jewish, Laz, Circassian, Arab and, above all, Turkish traditions. As a consequence, the history of rug weaving in Asia Minor is incredibly complex.

An early fifteenth-century miniature depicting Turkish nomads in their tents displays the prototypical nomadic weaving of Turkic peoples, with its simple geometric designs (plate 26). Although these very early patterns extend throughout the history of Turkish weaving, the rugs for which Anatolia has become famous, and which have long beguiled Western collectors, demonstrate very clearly the impact of the court tradition on village weaving. A splendid eighteenth-century rug from central Anatolia displays many of the characteristics of the weaving of the central plateau (plate 27). Comparatively narrow, because of the limitations of the small loom on which it was woven, it has a robust all-wool construction, a long and lustrous pile of primary colors enriched by a dark brown, and no more than two or three shoots of weft between each row of knots, which makes the pile tend to stand up fairly straight. The design, repetitious in nature, consists of medallions filled with stylized flowers in radially symmetrical

Colorplate 6.
Rugs from Milâs, in western Anatolia, were generally woven in the *sejjadeh* format, with soft wool and warm colors. This example from the late nineteenth century is distinguished by its exceptionally long pile and brilliant colors. 1850–1900. 173 x 111 cm. (5 ft. 8 in. x 3 ft. 8 in.). Fogg Art Museum, Cambridge, Mass.

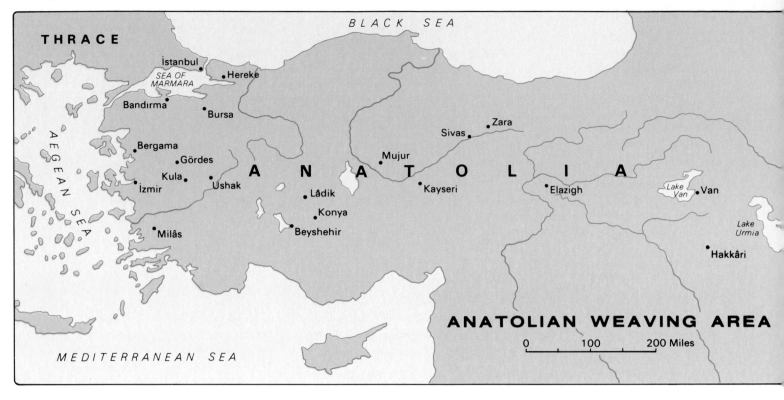

sprays, including tulips, carnations and hyacinths, the flowers most frequently seen in classical Ottoman art of the sixteenth century.

Another important element of Anatolian weaving is the great number of *sejjadeh*, or prayer rugs, woven in this part of the world. A prayer rug is a small rug, generally about one by one and a half meters in size, fit to provide the canonical "clean place" in which every devout Muslim is required by religious duty to prostrate himself in prayer. In practice, any rug, if clean, may be used for prayer, but the size of the *sejjadeh*, once established, led to the creation of a design particularly suitable for the purpose, although not all *sejjadeh* have it. The design is apparent in an example from the sixteenth-century Ottoman court workshops (plate 19, see page 35), where we see the *sejjadeh's* basic theme of an arch, probably echoing the mihrab, that niche in the wall of a Muslim communal prayer hall or mosque which faces the Holy City of Mecca. Turkish prayer rugs of succeeding centuries developed the basic theme of the arch, which in some sixteenth-century prayer rugs was accompanied by flanking columns and in others framed an unornamented field, into a variety of local types. The red-wefted and beautifully woven rugs from Milâs in western Asia Minor, for example, ornamented the central field with a few geometric forms but decorated the spandrels of the arch with stylized versions of the classical lotus palmette (plate 29).

Rugs woven in the area of the town of Lâdik in Konya province, on the other hand, show a design of long-stemmed tuliplike flowers growing over the spandrels above the unornamented prayer niche, the borders composed of sprays consisting of a single tulip flanked by two curved leaves (plate 28). The Lâdik rugs have an unusual construction, with the warp threads on two levels, which gives a characteristic corduroylike texture to the back of the rug. The nearby area of Mujur, producing prayer rugs whose designs show affinities with the Lâdik rugs, used different techniques, resulting in rugs which are much more flexible, and less strongly woven, than the Lâdik examples (colorplate 7). Such traditions of the individual types of rugs were deeply imbedded in their respective weaving localities until the advent of commercialization in the early twentieth century destroyed them.

The dislocations caused by the wars and internal strife in the Ottoman Empire in the latter part of the nineteenth century and the early twentieth all but obliterated any evidence of the stylistic changes that must have taken place and that might enable us to determine the provenance of past weaving on the basis of contemporary production. There is a tendency in the rug trade to use the nomenclature "Bergama" for any Anatolian rug of indeterminate provenance, but in fact it now appears that this term, stemming from the Turkish village on the site of classical Pergamon in western Anatolia, is an unfortunate misnomer. Scholars today tend to believe that central Anatolia, notably the area around the old thirteenth-century Seljuk capital city of Konya, was the production site of many of the most-admired examples of "Bergama" rugs (colorplate 8).

Sometimes, however, local traditions of weaving can be traced back to earlier types of rugs in a virtually unbroken chain. Turkish rugs of the so-called Transylvanian type (plate 30), found in great numbers in Rumanian and Hungarian churches, can be dated through European paintings to as early as the seventeenth century, while the rugs in the paintings themselves represent stylized adaptations of sixteenth-century court designs. The twentieth-century Anatolian village rug of the Yaghcıbehdir type (plate 31) echoes its eighteenth-century "Transylvanian" predecessor in its garland of white flowers and forklike stylized tulips around a centralized medallion, but the later rug is woven in an entirely different size, coloration and technique.

The presence of a vigorous tradition of folk mythology among rug-weaving peoples leaves open the question of symbolism in village weaving. In popular mythology in most Islamic lands, evil spirits may bring bad luck to one who possesses something coveted by the devil. Accordingly, small ornaments known as *nazarlık*, sometimes supplemented with tiny turquoise glass beads, were woven into rugs to ward off the minions of an envious devil. One side of popular religion in many Islamic lands was Sufi mysticism, the tendency to interpret

Muslim scriptures in symbolic and allegorical ways. Within this religious tradition, which looked upon forms existing in art and nature as reflections of divine ideas and ideals, symbolic meanings attached themselves to many of the forms seen in rugs. For instance, the arch on a prayer rug with an open field (colorplate 7) could be construed not as an architectural prayer niche but as the doorway to paradise, which is opened by the religious act of prayer. Filled with flowers (plate 19, see page 35), the arch becomes an actual representation of paradise itself, which in the Muslim Qur'an (Koran), or Holy Scriptures, is likened to a garden filled with softly murmuring brooks and flowering trees.

However, the apposition of a tradition of popular mythology and a commercial establishment which showed great imagination when it dealt with foreign collectors also led to the rise of "synthetic" myths about rugs. For example, abrash stripes in a rug (colorplate 9), potentially disconcerting to the Western buyer, were explained as "intentional flaws" deliberately introduced into the rug in order not to usurp the functions of the Almighty by creating a perfect thing. This

Colorplate 7.
The distinctive prayer rugs of Mujur (Mucur) in central Anatolia are generally woven starting from the top of the design, so that the pile leans toward the top of the mihrab niche. The bright colors and the two ewers flanking the niche are found in most Mujur rugs, which rarely appear in any except the *sejjadeh* format. Early nineteenth century. 185 x 137 cm. (6 ft. 1 in. x 4 ft. 6 in.). Private collection

26.
This early fifteenth-century miniature painting shows a tent decorated with textiles whose identical designs may still be found in Turkic nomadic tents throughout western and central Asia today. Topkapı Palace Museum, İstanbul

27

28

27.
The Konya district of Turkey, which seems to have produced some of the most interesting of all Anatolian village rugs, is evidently the point of origin of this lovely yellow-ground carpet. Eighteenth century. 415 x 120 cm. (13 ft. 8 in. x 3 ft. 11 in.). Rijksmuseum, Amsterdam

28.
The "classic" Lâdik rug, with its rich colors and vestigial triple-arch form, almost all of whose decorative motifs are directly derived from the late sixteenth-century Turkish prayer rugs, is probably the best known and most sought after of all Anatolian prayer rugs. Nineteenth century. 188 x 117 cm. (6 ft. 2 in. x 3 ft. 10 in.). St. Louis Art Museum, gift of James F. Ballard

29.
This western Anatolian *sejjadeh* from the Milâs district shows the persistence of classical Ottoman designs of the sixteenth century in village rug production. Nineteenth century. 148 x 107 cm. (4 ft. 10 in. x 3 ft. 6 in.). Fogg Art Museum, Cambridge, Mass.

29

charming invention would be plausible if one were able to detect in a considerable number of otherwise "perfect" rugs only one obtrusive "flaw" which gave the appearance of deliberate design. But for most village and nomadic weavings the fussy Western notions we may have of "perfection" simply do not apply. Therefore, one should not expect a Turkish village rug to articulate perfectly at the corners; in forming aesthetic criteria for looking at Anatolian village rugs, the notion of sophistication is best abandoned. A small central Anatolian prayer rug of undetermined provenance, with brilliant coloration, soft wool and an exquisite sense of color balance, charms the viewer on its own terms (see frontispiece), and meeting those terms is essential in order to develop a sense of the artistic accomplishments of these small masterpieces.

Flat-woven rugs were created in great abundance in many regions of Anatolia. In the west, simple brocaded rugs using red, white and blue on a red plain-weave foundation were quite common; slit-tapestry weaving was found throughout the area, giving way to *sumak* brocading in the east and northeast. The limitations of loom width often meant that large *kilim* rugs were woven in two strips and then joined, although sometimes differences in the warp structure will cause one side to shrink more than the other. In a particularly magnificent example of a large central Anatolian *kilim* (plate 32), the colors range from a deep vermilion to a sky blue, and the whites are woven in bleached cotton, which provides sharp accents in the overall diapered design. From the Afshar area of Kayseri province, settled in medieval times according to tradition by Turkish peoples from Central Asia, come large *kilim* rugs woven in one piece. The most exciting of these great rugs, with their strong horizontal interlockings dictated by the technique, combine the medallion form with a host of tiny geometrical ornaments in a fashion reminiscent of the early carpets of the Caucasus (colorplate 10). In some *kilim* weaving from Turkey one can still see vestiges of the sixteenth-century classical style which, despite its lack of suitability to the geometric technique of the slit-tapestry weave, has managed to maintain its influence over the village weavers (plate 33).

The *sejjadeh*, as we have noted, was the most frequently encountered Anatolian format. Comparing a splendid *sejjadeh* rug from the Milâs district with no mihrab (colorplate 6) with its counterpart which has one (plate 29), we can see that the difference in terms of design between a "prayer rug" and a small rug of prayer-rug dimensions is frequently quite minimal.

Another format much loved in Anatolian weaving was the *yastık*, or cushion rug (generally about 60 x 100 cm.), actually used for a multitude of functions. With its backing, it formed a sack which could either be stuffed and used as a cushion to line the earthen benches which constituted the furniture of the *sofa* (reception room)

Colorplate 8.
One of the "Bergama" rugs probably actually woven in the district around the old Seljuk capital of Konya, this example is distinguished by its great regularity of weaving. The wide border with its design of heavily stylized lotus flowers on a yellow ground is derived from a seventeenth-century Persian prototype, but all the curvilinear qualities of the original have disappeared and the brilliant colors have come to dominate the visual impression. Nineteenth century. Dimensions not given. Private collection

Colorplate 9.
Gördes, in western Anatolia, produced prayer rugs in characteristic pale colors and intricate designs which attained great popularity in Europe. This example, with abrash plainly visible in its pale green open field mihrab, typifies Gördes weaving at its best. About 1800–1850. 195 x 135 cm. (6 ft. 5 in. x 4 ft. 5 in.). George Walter Vincent Smith Art Museum, Springfield, Mass.

COLORPLATE 8

COLORPLATE 9

30

31

30.
"Transylvanian" rugs like this one, with its garland of flowers surrounding a central medallion, serve as the prototypes for a much later western Anatolian rug known as a Yaghcıbehdir. Late eighteenth century. 161 x 119 cm. (5 ft. 3½ in. x 3 ft. 11 in.). Metropolitan Museum of Art, New York, bequest of Joseph V. McMullan, 1974

31.
The small rugs of western Anatolia, with their wide bands of *kilim* at each end and their distinctive end finishes, sometimes reflect earlier designs. In the case of the small rugs known as Yaghcıbehdirs, the model is a particular type of "Transylvanian" rug known to have been woven as early as the eighteenth century. Early twentieth century. 121 x 105 cm. (4 ft. x 3 ft. 6 in.). Private collection

in a Turkish village house or left free to hold wheat, barley or some other dry provision. Without the backing, these little rugs were used as covers for furniture or as saddles, or were incorporated into leather bags, packsaddles and horse trappings. Some *yastık* designs reflected simpler textiles (plate 36); others adapted the medallion format of their larger cousins and displayed at each end the row of niches, or lappets, which traditionally formed the ends of silk velvet cushion covers in sixteenth- and seventeenth-century court-designed textiles of Bursa (plate 34).

In contrast to the brilliantly colored weavings of the Anatolian west coast and central plateau, the western towns of Gördes and Kula produced astonishing numbers of *sejjadeh* rugs in markedly subtle colors (colorplate 9 and plate 35). These soft color schemes adapted especially well to that eighteenth-century period taste virtually synonymous with elegance in both the Western and the Ottoman Turkish upper-class world of the nineteenth century. The phenomenal success of these rugs on Western markets, and the relatively high prices they brought at sales, inspired a host of imitators, and rugs in the Gördes design were made not only at Bandırma on the Sea of

32.
This large *kilim* of central Anatolia, woven in two pieces, is unusual in the clarity of its colors, the use of metallic thread, cotton and silk in addition to the traditional wool, and the inclusion of a small, unfortunately unreadable poem in Turkish hidden in one compartment of the diapered design. Nineteenth century. 395 x 146 cm. (12 ft. 11 in. x 4 ft. 10 in.). Museum of Fine Arts, Boston, Ross Collection

33

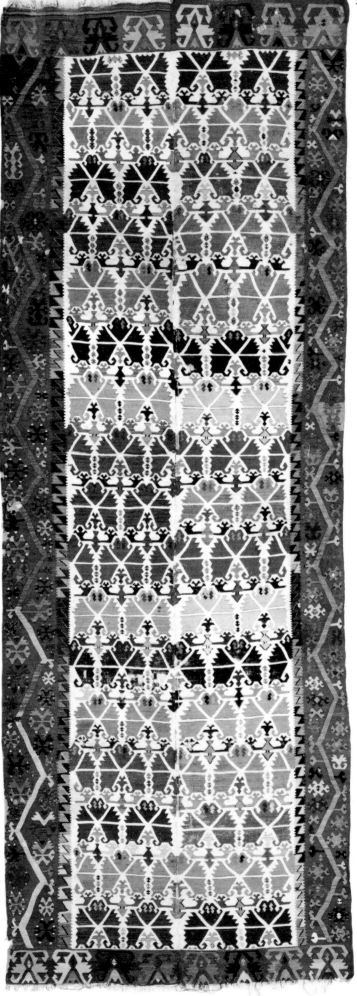

34

35

33.
The stylized flowers beloved of sixteenth-century Turkish artists live on in this nineteenth-century tapestry-woven rug from Anatolia. Stacked row upon row, the fanlike carnations are all but lost in the geometry of the weaving technique. Nineteenth century. 448 x 164 cm. (14 ft. 8 in. x 5 ft. 5 in.). Collection Alexander and Helen Philon, London

34.
Distinguished by the row of small arch-like forms, or lappets, at each end, this little Anatolian *yastık* from the Konya area manages to sport a dominating medallion, while vestiges of stylized carnations may be seen in the corners. Nineteenth century. 101 x 60 cm. (3 ft. 4 in. x 2 ft.). Private collection

35.
Kula, in western Asia Minor, like its sister town of Gördes was distinguished in the nineteenth century for its production of prayer rugs in muted colors. In this example the columns of the mihrab have evolved into two decorative bands, while the lamp representing the lamps of the mosque, which hangs under the arch, has become a stylized vase of flowers. Nineteenth century. 158 x 112 cm. (5 ft. 2 in. x 3 ft. 8 in.). George Walter Vincent Smith Art Museum, Springfield, Mass.

36.
Zara, a weaving center to the east of Sivas in central Anatolia, is apparently the place of origin of this small Turkish *yastık*, with its characteristic design of a meandering vine on multicolored stripes in which maroon and very dark yellow predominate. About 1900. Approximate size: 90 x 45 cm. (3 ft. x 1½ ft.). George Walter Vincent Smith Art Museum, Springfield, Mass.

Marmara and Kayseri on the central Anatolian plateau but in locations as remote as Tabriz in Persian Azerbaijan.

It is impossible to characterize Anatolian rugs technically beyond a few broad generalizations. In most cases, the range of colors used tends to be rather wide and concentrates on highly saturated primary and secondary hues, which in the best examples exhibit a tremendous sense of balance and harmony. Most Anatolian rugs are made entirely of wool—they have a woolen pile on a woolen warp and weft. Exceptions are found in commercial manufactories, which were prominent in Anatolian weaving as early as the second half of the nineteenth century; rugs produced commercially near Kayseri and Sivas and in Hereke near Istanbul, for example, are more likely to be woven on cotton warp and weft, with silk, mercerized cotton or even rayon being used in some examples. Also, most Anatolian village pile rugs are constructed with a symmetrical, or Turkish, knot, and it is unusual to find an example with more than about 2300 knots to the square decimeter (150 to the square inch).

Turkey's proximity to Europe, a tremendous asset in previous centuries when the Ushak factories were exporting large quantities of Turkish carpets to western Europe through Italian middlemen, brought a terrible calamity on the world of the Turkish rug in the latter part of the nineteenth century, when western Anatolia was first in the Islamic orient to feel the impact of cheap aniline dyes produced in Europe. Because of the great ease with which aniline dyeing could be accomplished, these dyes spread like wildfire. Since they were usually improperly used, they produced a blighted generation of rugs which were unable to hold their colors and in which hues

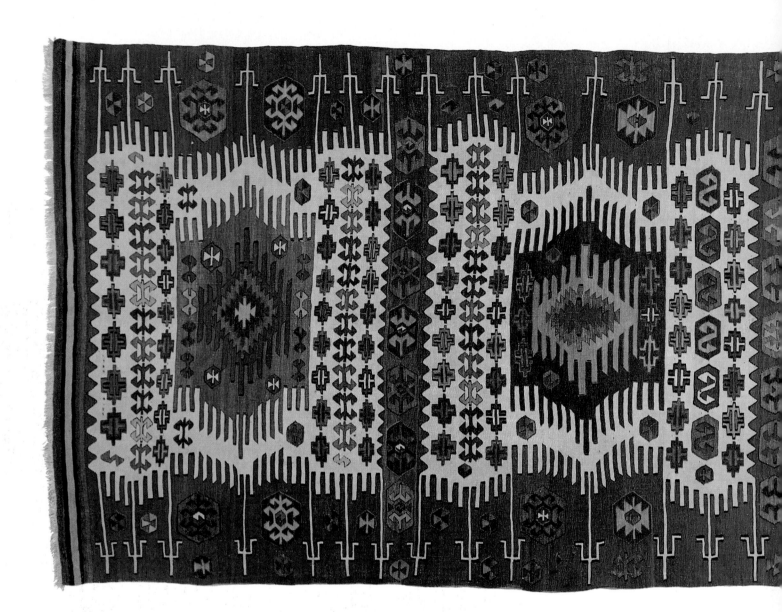

Colorplate 10.
The large tapestry-woven rugs of central
Anatolia show a wide variety of designs,
with the bold *kilims* of the Afshar district
of Kayseri province, as here, displaying
some of the most spectacular. 1850–1900.
332 x 171 cm. (10 ft. 11 in. x 5 ft. 7 in.).
Private collection

entirely foreign to the exquisite color sense of Turkish weaving quickly swamped the older traditions. The foulest of these invaders from the West was a particularly obnoxious purple, which mercifully often faded to a completely neutral dirty gray or beige. On the other hand, another popular hue was a metallic orange which appears to maintain its unnerving intensity through every vicissitude that can befall a rug short of burning. While in certain parts of Anatolia rug weaving continues under the aegis of older traditions, the aniline blight remains in many areas today.

Contemporary Turkish weaving is a curious mixture of neotraditionalism and modern entrepreneurial capitalism. The monotonous flowered rugs of Kayseri, certainly an adequate form of floor covering, are rarely encountered in Western markets. Small all-wool village rugs from the south and west coasts are now increasingly appearing in American markets, and the Yaghcıbehdirs and Döshemealtıs, together with the central Anatolian Yahyahlıs and Tashpınars, provide pleasing geometric scatter rugs whose designs and colors are approximations of the traditional patterns of the past. The Kula factory near İzmir has produced excellently woven reproductions of many of the traditional types, which, although certainly no substitute for the Lâdiks, Mujurs and Gördeses of past times, at least have the attractive feature that they can be walked upon without risking desecration of a major work of village art. Certain eastern districts, most prominently the areas around Van and Hakkâri, continue to produce pile rugs and flat-woven *kilims* which are worthy descendants of earlier traditional weaving; in marked contrast are today's Milâs rugs, pale beige and gray ghosts of those gloriously colored red-wefted rugs which once made the name of Milâs famous.

4 Rugs of the Caucasus

Few geographical areas of the world present more geological and ethnological complexity in a small area than does the Caucasus (map 3, see page 60). In this region between the Black Sea on the west and the Caspian on the east, with its twin backbones of the Lesser and Greater Caucasus mountain ranges and its fertile coastal plains and great valleys, we find Turks and Georgians, Armenians and Persians, Kurds and Slavs mixed together in a bewildering pattern of nomadic, village and urban ways of life. As a meeting ground of East and West, Christendom and Islam, orthodox Turkey and heterodox Persia, and the fiercely independent cultural traditions of Georgia and Armenia, the Caucasus presents us with a weaving tradition of great richness and diversity.

The oldest pile-woven rugs from the Caucasus are the so-called dragon carpets, the earliest of which are datable to the seventeenth century (colorplate 12). These large rugs, already heavily stylized in design, clearly reflect the influence of the art and symbology of China on the Islamic world, although their immediate models were probably Persian rugs with Chinese designs woven in central Iran. The stylized and simplified motifs of the dragon fighting with the phoenix, the lion with flames springing from its shoulders and the curious antelopelike creature known as the *chi'lin* are, even in the earliest examples, immediately recognizable only to the specialist, since the forms are under the spell of the geometric medium of the loom. It is precisely this geometric simplification, with its craggy outlines and bold patterning, coupled with brilliant colors, that gives the early dragon rugs their extraordinary visual power and excitement.

Among these early dragon rugs appear a few examples with inscriptions in the Armenian language, evidence of the importance of the patronage of an Armenian moneyed merchant class in the Caucasus from early times but not, as once thought, evidence that the rugs

Colorplate 11.
Among the rarest of Caucasian rugs, the small and exceptionally finely woven prayer rugs of the eastern Caucasus, with almost 4650 knots to the square decimeter (300 to the square inch) on a blue ground, are of uncertain date and provenance, although the Shirvan district has been suggested as a place of origin. This example includes silk in the pile at irregular intervals. Nineteenth century. 132 x 115 cm. (4 ft. 4 in. x 3 ft. 9 in.). Fogg Art Museum, Cambridge, Mass.

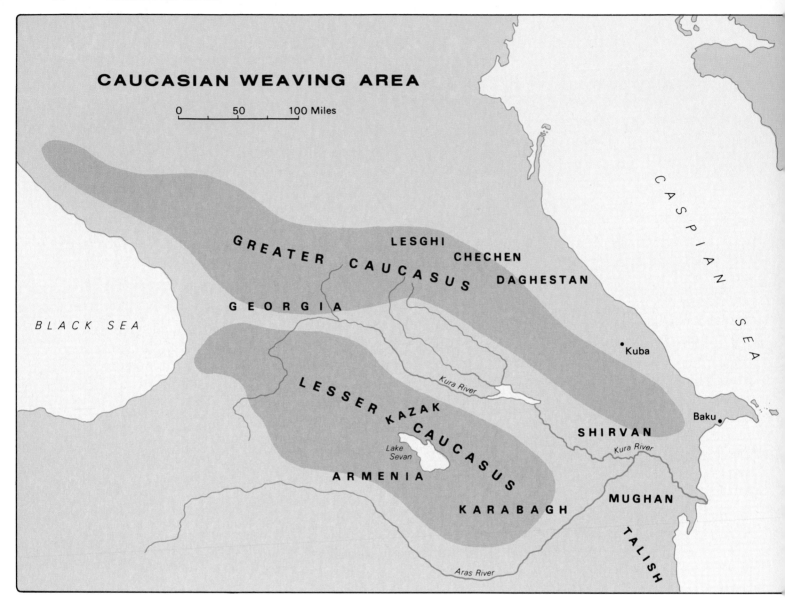

CAUCASIAN WEAVING AREA

0   50   100 Miles

CASPIAN SEA

GREATER CAUCASUS

LESGHI
CHECHEN
DAGHESTAN

GEORGIA

BLACK SEA

Kuba

LESSER KAZAK CAUCASUS

Kura River

SHIRVAN

Baku

Lake Sevan

ARMENIA

KARABAGH

Kura River

MUGHAN

TALISH

Aras River

constituted an Armenian art form. The bulk of these early Caucasian rugs, at one time commonly called Kuba carpets in the trade, appear to have been woven in the central and southern Caucasus as commercial products, comparable in their genesis to the Ushak carpets of western Turkey. Their shape generally tends to be long and narrow, with examples up to six meters in length frequently encountered. A wide range of basic hues was employed in bold combinations and large-scale repeating patterns, rendered almost invariably in the symmetrical, or Turkish, knot in woolen pile on an all-wool foundation.

The influence of the dragon carpets continued to be felt even when

Colorplate 12.
With its bright greens and yellows on a vivid red ground, this cut-down turn-of-the-seventeenth-century rug is one of the most attractive members of the Caucasian dragon carpet family to have survived. The general design type is the most frequently encountered in dragon carpets, with each of the major motifs occurring only twice in the carpet. About 1700. 358 x 175 cm. (11 ft. 9 in. x 5 ft. 9 in.). Textile Museum, Washington, D.C.

Caucasian rug weaving moved from the commercial manufactories to the village looms. Indeed, few rugs of the seventeenth century exercised as great an influence on their stylistic progeny as did the dragon carpets, and motifs from the early rugs were still abstracted and used in countless village and nomadic rugs when the volume of production of small rugs in the Caucasus reached its peak in the early twentieth century.

The village and nomadic Caucasian rugs of the nineteenth and early twentieth centuries are generally grouped under geographical rubrics; from the south came the loosely woven long-piled rugs of the Karabagh district (plate 37); the mountainous Lesser Caucasus was the point of origin of the long-piled, red-wefted, often shaggy Kazak rugs, with their bold designs and colors (colorplate 13 and plate 38). From the upper end of the Kura valley came rugs of more subtle coloration and greater intricacy of design, frequently influenced by European (Russian) taste (plate 39), while on the Shirvan coastal plain on the Caspian were woven the more brilliantly colored rugs of the Shirvan rubric (plate 40) and, on the coast to the south, the long, narrow rugs of the Talish and Mughan areas (plate 42). Northward on the Caspian shore is the Kuba district, where more finely woven rugs (colorplate 15) from a variety of villages originated, as did cotton-warped commercial rugs in the eighteenth and nineteenth centuries. From the northern Caucasus, in the mountainous region called Daghestan, came short-piled rugs from various mountain peoples, such as the Chechen and Lesghi tribal groups (plates 41 and 44). All these rugs, with very few exceptions, shared several common features: a wide range of brilliant colors; designs showing a multitude of origins but usually bearing in some way the stamp of the seventeenth-century dragon carpets; and a symmetrical, or Turkish, knot. Within this broad area of common ground, moreover, we find an almost bewildering variety of common designs and weaving techniques brought about by extensive borrowings of designs and widespread use of the same mass-produced yarns. These factors, together with a breakdown in the particularistic application of tribal and religious symbols, helped to blur the distinctions between the various rug groupings.

The most easily recognizable of all Caucasian rugs are the Kazaks. Kazak rugs as a group are coarsely woven, usually with a long pile, and as a consequence tend to have extremely bold, large-scale designs. The best examples show brilliant coloration and wool of great softness and light-reflectivity. The most authoritative scholarship assigns to Kazak rugs a red-dyed weft, which appears in discernible horizontal stripes on the flat back of the rug, and a very "meaty" feel. These mountain village weavings exhibit some of the most powerful designs and colorations to be found in the Caucasus, and even those designs peculiar to the most humble village appear to have roots in the distant

Colorplate 13.
A common Caucasian design, the small stepped medallion with "hooked" angles, appears in this heavy-piled Kazak rug. Also typical of village weaving in the southern Caucasus are the rug's brilliant colors and the sometimes awkward adjustments of details of the design. Nineteenth century. 173 x 139 cm. (5 ft. 8 in. x 4 ft. 7 in.). Allen Memorial Art Museum, Oberlin, Ohio, gift of Charles M. Hall

Colorplate 14.
In this Kazak rug, certainly among the largest of the village rugs of the southern Caucasus, the brilliantly colored red field is contained by a border in which remains of the early Kufic borders can be seen in greatly simplified form. Like most rugs from the Kazak district, this one only roughly approximates a rectilinear outline because of the crowding together of warps at the upper end of the loom. Nineteenth century. 244 x 180 cm. (8 ft. x 5 ft. 11 in.). Metropolitan Museum of Art, New York, bequest of Joseph V. McMullan, 1973

37

38

37.
The so-called eagle Kazak rugs were actually woven in the Karabagh area of the
southeastern Caucasus. With their designs of white medallions on a red ground,
they have long been perhaps the most
sought-after village rugs, collectors of all
nations having paid unprecedented prices
to obtain fine examples. Nineteenth century. 194 x 130 cm. (6 ft. 5 in. x 4 ft. 3
in.). Museum of Applied Arts, Budapest

38.
This well-known type of Kazak rug
combines the central focus of Persian
medallion carpets with the rugged geometric forms and heavy, even shaggy,
pile of southern Caucasian rugs. Second
half of the nineteenth century. 200 x 140
cm. (6 ft. 7 in. x 4 ft. 7 in.). Museum of
Applied Arts, Budapest

past. For example, one of the best-known types of Kazak rug has a
two-one-two disposition of medallions (plate 38) which beyond
any doubt stems from the large-patterned Holbeins of the early
sixteenth century.

Another characteristic of rug designs of the Caucasus is the use of a
single motif, or a part of a motif, from an earlier design in a fashion
totally abstracted from its original context. It is in this manner that in
a rug from the Kazak area a curved leaf from an earlier prototype has
taken on a completely stylized form, its veins represented by tiny
yellow crescents (colorplate 14). Here the weaver, using her exquisite
sense of balance and color, has created a masterpiece of design whose
awkward corner adjustments merely underline the charm of the Kazak
weavers' casual approach to symmetry and draftsmanship (see also
colorplate 13).

The southeastern Caucasus, the "black garden," or Karabagh district, seems to have been more susceptible to foreign types of design

39.

Rugs from the southwestern Caucasus of this type, with their oddly Europeanized curvilinear ornaments, form a curious contrast with the more geometric rugs of the Kazak area. On a light blue ground, this particularly lovely example has a characteristic border, derived from stylized representations of flowers, that is sometimes called a Greek Wave design for reasons that are obscure. Late nineteenth century. 264 x 102 cm. (8 ft. 8 in. x 3 ft. 4 in.). George Walter Vincent Smith Art Museum, Springfield, Mass.

40.

A design of stylized lotus palmettes abstracted from either a Persian prototype or a dragon rug dominates the narrow center field of this Shirvan rug, with its "crab border" of rosettes in repeat. A wide range of intense colors characterizes this example, and indeed is typical of most eastern Caucasian rugs. Late nineteenth century. 275 x 112 cm. (9 ft. x 3 ft. 8 in.). George Walter Vincent Smith Art Museum, Springfield, Mass.

COLORPLATE 15

COLORPLATE 16

than the rest of the Caucasus. Adaptations of many Persian design types are found there, among which the most charming are the vase carpets modeled ultimately after seventeenth-century central Persian rugs (colorplate 27, see page 114).

The best-known Karabagh rugs are those called, in the trade, eagle or sunburst rugs, once erroneously thought to belong to the Kazak family (plate 37). The power of the craggy white medallions, whose rootlike extensions thrust out into the surrounding field, has no doubt contributed to the popularity of this design with collectors. The design itself may represent ultimately the rationalization and "radialization" of a floral form from an earlier prototype; it occurs in a less developed form on many large slit-tapestry-woven Caucasian rugs, which were in turn copied, down to the interlocking along the verticals, in a few very rare pile-woven carpets from the Shirvan district, where the "sunburst" medallion appears in a smaller and less powerful form (plate 43). Rugs from the Shirvan littoral proper show the finer Shirvan weave and lower pile, resulting in designs of much greater complexity (plate 40). Shirvan rugs as a rule were woven on narrow looms and tend to be from two to three times as long as wide, except for those in the *sejjadeh* format.

The Talish and Mughan rugs of the southeastern Caucasus were apparently woven in very small numbers. The unusual designs of the long, narrow Talish rugs (plate 42) have great appeal for collectors, and since the rugs are so few they command very high prices whenever they appear on the market. Less is known of Mughan weavings, in which often brilliant, Kazak-like coloration is combined with a medium-density weave and a medium-length pile.

One of the most commonly encountered types of Caucasian rug is the prayer rug of fine weave from the eastern and northern Caucasus. In certain areas prayer rugs tended to incorporate some of the area's most characteristic and persistent village designs, so that attribution of prayer rugs to particular groups of weavers is often relatively easy to accomplish. Rugs from both the Kuba area and the mountains of Daghestan in the north were woven in relatively fine knotting, with a corresponding very short pile, which made the element of draftsmanship more important than it was in the color-dominated southern Caucasian rugs. A prayer rug from the Kuba area uses the Persian device of the *boteh*, probably a stylized leaf, in its field (colorplate 15). The interstices of the design have been filled with depictions of a camel, a dog, a bow and arrow and two types of pitchers in common use in the late nineteenth and early twentieth centuries in the Caucasus. The best of these Kuba rugs, as often as not woven with a cotton weft, are, in the wealth of their detail and the charm of those arbitrary examples of the weavers' imaginations that fill the interstices of their designs, among the most visually interesting of Caucasian rugs.

Colorplate 15.
A design of rows of *boteh* forms, no two exactly alike, decorates this *sejjadeh* rug from the Kuba district of the Caucasus; its border design is shared with certain rugs woven by Yomud Turkoman tribes on the eastern shore of the Caspian. The rose-colored ground is unusual in rugs of this type, but the prayer-rug format is among the most common of Kuba weavings. Late nineteenth century. 154 x 134 cm. (5 ft. x 4 ft. 5 in.). Private collection

Colorplate 16.
The large-patterned Holbein design survives in this *sumak*-brocaded rug from the eastern Caucasus, but the village weaver has used her own imagination in filling in the field with various bits of traditional design. Nineteenth century. 173 x 137 cm. (5 ft. 8 in. x 4 ft. 6 in.). George Walter Vincent Smith Art Museum, Springfield, Mass.

41.
Chechen, or Chichi, tribal weavings from
the northern Caucasus closely resemble
the prayer rugs of the eastern Caucasian
littoral in their general size and disposition of motifs. The characteristic border,
derived from a series of long diagonally
placed leaves, and the dark blue ground
distinguish this small prayer rug as a
Chechen rug. Late nineteenth century.
158 x 124 cm. (5 ft. 2 in. x 4 ft. 1 in.).
Private collection

42.
An anomaly among oriental rugs, the
characteristic Talish rug of the southeastern Caucasus has a dark blue center
field totally devoid of ornament, with
only the fluctuating colors of the mono-
chromatic field, caused by abrash, giving
a subtle variety to the restful void. Late
nineteenth century. 247 x 107 cm. (8 ft.
1 in. x 3 ft. 3 in.). Anonymous collection

42

41

Sometimes the basic element abstracted from an earlier rug so
dominates the field of a rug that the use of "fillers" is almost impossible. Such is the case with a variety of long rugs from various parts
of the northern Caucasus which utilize a huge calyx form taken from
eighteenth-century carpets of the southern Caucasus (plate 44).

The Chechen tribal group of the northern Caucasus, which acquired
the memorable name of Chichi in the Western rug market, seems to
have clung more tenaciously than other Caucasian groups to a particular type of design, a distinctive border marked by a diagonal "bar,"
the ultimate stylization of a curved leaf (plate 41).

The general format of northern Caucasian prayer rugs appears in
a small number of eastern Caucasian rugs of surpassingly fine weave,
whose specific geographical origin remains unknown (colorplate 11).
Woven with a precision not commonly encountered in the Caucasus,
these small prayer rugs use the most exquisitely fine wool, often
enhanced with gleaming bits of silk.

Like the weavers of Anatolia to the west, the Caucasian weavers
delighted in making flat-woven rugs of all sorts; but whereas the
Anatolian plateau favored the slit-tapestry-woven rug, or *kilim*, in the

43.
Occasionally the borrowing of designs from rugs of one technique by rugs of another can be clearly detected. This design, by the interlocking edges of its forms, betrays its origin in slit-tapestry weave, but the rug is in fact a pile-woven carpet from the Shirvan district of the eastern Caucasus. Nineteenth century. Dimensions not given. Collection Raoul and Ingeborg Tschebull, Frankfurt am Main, West Germany

Caucasus the brocaded *sumak* appears to have been the favored form. It is often in *sumak* weaving, which seems to have been concentrated in the Shirvan area and points south, that one finds some of the most traditional of Caucasian designs, such as the large-patterned Holbein medallions (colorplate 16). Another characteristic type of *sumak* brocading in the Caucasus is the large brocaded cover known in the trade as a *sileh* (plate 45).

One may say with some justification that the *sumak* weavers of the southern Caucasus, northwestern Persia and extreme eastern Anatolia have produced not only the largest number of weavings in the technique but also many of the outstanding masterpieces of the medium. Southward in the territory of the Shah Sevan ("those who love the king"), we find in the nineteenth century a substantial production of *sumak*-brocaded pieces in a variety of "small formats," including the *heybe*, or *khorjin*, small double bags meant to be used as saddle-bags though sometimes carried over the shoulder (plate 46). These small but often exquisitely beautiful pieces were frequently cut apart for the Western market, and today many small bag faces exist without their partners or their backing and laces. Another form of weaving from this area is the so-called box bag (plate 47). In many examples,

44.
The tendency of later Caucasian rugs to abstract a single motif from earlier carpets and use it in repeat is seen in this extraordinary carpet from the Lesghi region in the northern Caucasus, whose lustrous wool and intense, rich colors are dominated by a gigantic calyx form in repeat. Late nineteenth century. 300 x 114 cm. (9 ft. 10 in. x 3 ft. 9 in.). Detail (half). Fogg Art Museum, Cambridge, Mass.

45.
The ubiquitous Chinese dragon appears
in repeat on this *sileh* flat-woven *sumak*-
brocaded rug from the Caucasus. These
geometric dragons are flying with their
tails high in the air, and the bottom extensions of the backward-*S* shapes represent their lower jaws. Nineteenth century. 270 x 190 cm. (8 ft. 10 in. x 6 ft.
3 in.). Österreichisches Museum für angewandte Kunst, Vienna

the four sides are woven in *sumak* technique, while the bottom is
weft-faced plain weave. Bags of this sort very rarely appear in the
West intact but instead have been cut into pieces and the faces made
into pillow covers or table runners.

The impact of Western markets on the traditional weaving of the
Caucasus is still to be studied in detail, but it seems that Caucasian
weaving was badly affected by the appearance of aniline dyes in the
Near East in the late nineteenth century. There exist entire classes of
Caucasian rugs which were originally dyed with fugitive reds and
purples that have faded to beige and gray respectively. These, however, are much in demand today as complements to European period
furniture because of their un-Islamic coloration. Moreover, in certain
parts of the Caucasus, most notably the oil-soaked area of Baku, were
woven late nineteenth-century carpets with an overall design of large

46.
Long since separated from its twin and
the plain-weave strip that formed the
back of the double saddlebag it was once
part of, this little *sumak*-brocaded bag
face with its variety of traditional Caucasian motifs represents a type of weaving
in tremendous demand among collectors;
fine examples are rarely encountered and
command staggering prices. Late nineteenth century. 61 x 61 cm. (2 ft. x 2 ft.).
Fogg Art Museum, Cambridge, Mass.

47.
Box bags were known under a variety of
names but served a common purpose as
containers for quilts and other bulky
items of bedding. This example, woven
in *sumak* brocading, is thought to have
been made by Shah Sevan women in
northwestern Iran or the extreme northeastern corner of Turkey. Early twentieth century. 105 x 44 x 51 cm. (41⅜ x
17⅜ x 20 in.). Private collection

46

47

boteh forms whose subdued coloration no doubt has contributed to their appeal in the West (plate 48).

In the 1920s, during the period of resurgent capitalism under what was known as the New Economic Policy, the Soviet Government sponsored a revival of rug weaving in the Caucasus, the purpose being to produce rugs of very high quality in the best traditions of Caucasian folk art that could be sold abroad to raise much needed foreign exchange. Rugs of this period in Caucasian weaving are often of the very highest weaving quality, using carefully controlled dyes and exhibiting designs of the purest and most impeccable authenticity. Here, however, it is the very perfection of these late Caucasian products which, in the eyes of some collectors at least, tends to detract from their beauty and charm. But to many other collectors, these reproductions of earlier Caucasian weaving are extremely appealing, and in certain cases have assumed a place in the ranks of nineteenth-century Caucasian weaving as a consequence. In the Caucasus today rugs are still woven as part of a conscious attempt to continue older folk-art forms and to preserve the national identities of the various Caucasian peoples through perpetuation of traditional crafts. The Armenian Soviet Socialist Republic has been the most active in this area, but the rugs, while stemming from the sincerest of motives, are all too often a reflection of tastes in which "perfection" triumphs over the relaxed and even disorderly artistic genius of the Caucasian village weaver of the nineteenth century.

48.
Although we generally think of later Caucasian rugs as being produced in small format, the weavers of the Baku district not only used the curvilinear *boteh* forms of Persian design but followed the larger sizes of Persian carpets as well. In another deviation, the large Baku carpets display colors more restrained than those thought typical of Caucasian weaving. Nineteenth century. 389 x 168 cm. (12 ft. 9 in. x 5 ft. 6 in.). Anonymous collection

COLORPLATE 17

COLORPLATE 18

5   Rugs of Iran

Certainly when one thinks of rugs no area of the world comes to mind more quickly than Persia (map 4, see page 76). The great Persian carpets of the sixteenth and seventeenth centuries were the standards toward which the entire carpet-weaving world once looked, and in the Western world, where floor covering has been the primary use for rugs, the large Persian carpet and its cousins the smaller "area rugs" have long been familiar. And yet the rubric Persian rug is once again a term of convenience only, as the variety of weaving found in the land known today as Iran is in some respects even more vast than that found in Turkey or the Caucasus. As the result of a dramatic increase in commercial weaving in Persia around 1860, the Persian rugs most commonly seen in the West are products made after that date. Spearheaded by the merchants of Tabriz in northwestern Persia, who had developed excellent commercial contacts with Europe, the production of rugs in sizes and shapes suitable for Western floor covering spread from the Tabriz area to other major carpet-making centers in Iran, such as the Hamadan, Arak and Kerman weaving areas. Despite the dominance of commercial weaving in Iran, and the resultant cleavage between traditional and commercial weaving which penetrated to the village level in Persia more than a century ago, however, large numbers of traditional nomadic carpets, whose production remained little touched by commercialism until relatively modern times, have continued to be woven by the nomadic peoples of Iran.

While the village rug production of Turkey and the Caucasus remained largely true to the traditional *sejjadeh* sizes and local designs established before any influence of Western markets was felt, in Iran after 1860 village weaving for the most part very quickly adapted through economic necessity to a market which preferred "room-sized carpets," "runners" and "area rugs." Commercial production brought a system of sizes, falling generally within the rubrics "eight by ten

Colorplate 17.
With its many tiny designs scattered across the field, this Qashqai rug from Fars is typical of the nomadic weaving of southern Persia. Late nineteenth century. 218 x 176 cm. (7 ft. 2 in. x 5 ft. 9 in.). Fogg Art Museum, Cambridge, Mass.

Colorplate 18.
Iranian rugs of this coloration have long been called "Laver" Kermans, "Laver" being a corruption of Ravar, the name of the town near Kerman where they were supposedly woven, although there is little evidence to connect them with the town. This example is unusual in its excellent state of preservation, and the slightly Europeanized ornateness of its design represents an accommodation of traditions of Persian design to the Western rug market. Early twentieth century. 437 x 315 cm. (14 ft. 4 in. x 10 ft. 4 in.). Collection Mr. and Mrs. Levon C. Register, Chattanooga

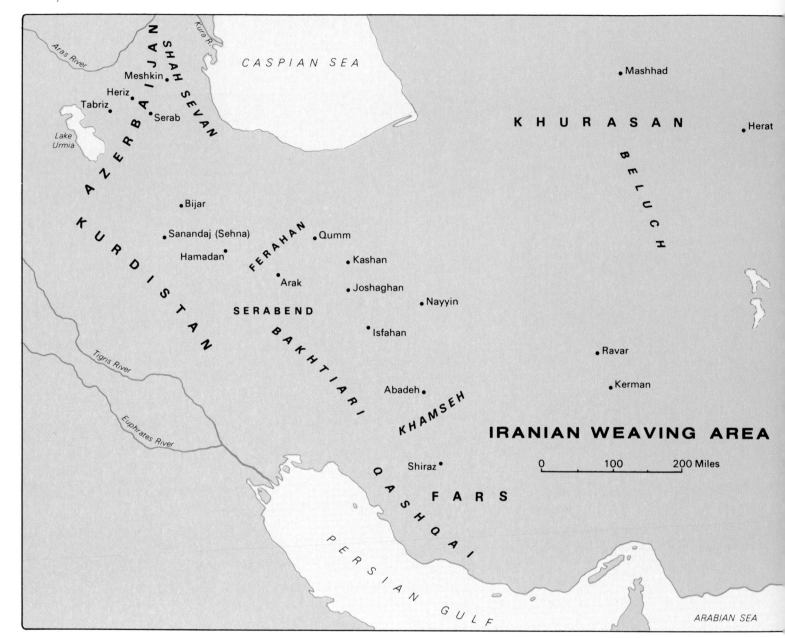

feet," "nine by twelve feet" and "ten by fourteen feet," and a standard system of grades, with corresponding price structures. Although much of Persian rug production therefore accommodated itself to a commercial structure, age-old village traditions persisted to a degree and occasionally manifested themselves in various ways in the supposedly "controlled" final product. But in many Persian rugs we find prestige and costliness relate primarily to the *technical* quality and fineness of the rug, and as a consequence a large number were woven in anticipation of the heavy everyday use they would find in Western households, where the barbarous habits of the natives included the wearing of street shoes in the house.

Because Persian rugs fall generally into technically established groupings (within which there are variances in design which affect their attractiveness in a Western market) and are priced accordingly, many were, and still are, marketed on a "per square foot" basis at a standard price determined by density of knotting and wearability of materials used. And while, to be sure, two rugs from the same village woven in the same density and with the same wearability might exhibit individual characteristics of design making one a masterpiece and the other a visual disaster, collectors have found that the market for Persian rugs is in general far more uniform, and the value of a given rug type more easily established, than for other types of rugs. Such standardization, coupled with the large size and basically utilitarian purpose of so many Persian rugs, meant that until comparatively recently only the smaller, very finely woven examples were likely to have been considered "collector's items," and many a very beautiful, but loosely woven, example was held in relative contempt.

By examining the literature on Persian rugs woven during the last one hundred years, which draws upon the excellent documentation available from commercial sources and takes advantage of the great interest shown in establishing provenance as a factor in sales prices, one is able to distinguish the rug production of extremely small localized areas with relative ease, down to the product of a particular loom in a particular village. In the present discussion we will consider the weaving of rugs in Persia by geographical area in a somewhat broader fashion, keeping in mind that terminology in Persian weaving may refer to (1) the geographical point of origin of a rug, (2) the nature of the design of a rug or (3) the particular grade or technical quality of a rug. The confusion of these variables in the market may sometimes be to the buyer's disadvantage, as the names of weaving areas with considerable magic such as Tabriz, Kashan, Kerman and Isfahan may be applied to rugs whose designs are only derivatives of these famous prototypes or to rugs made in the same neighborhood but whose quality of weaving is in no way comparable. In the same way, however, there are certain named varieties of Persian rugs that possess very little market prestige but of which occasional examples occur of great beauty and of great interest to the collector.

The commercial organization of the production of some of the more recent Persian rugs has resulted in some practices directed toward the taste of the Western buyer. For example, earlier in this century large numbers of so-called Sarouk and Lilahan rugs from the Arak district were chemically treated in order to remove a commercially unsuccessful bright red ground color and subsequently "painted" with a more "appealing" plum red and navy blue. Enormous quantities of rugs in this coloration are to be found in the West, and while many make excellent floor coverings, one must avoid dealing with them as original products of folk art, so drastically has their appearance been altered. It was the control of Persian village looms by Western retail merchants that led, in Persia more than in any other rug-weaving area, to a market responsiveness on the part of the weavers which in many cases destroyed any claim their rugs might have had to being a type of folk art rooted in native traditions. The "pastel Kerman" rugs of the 1950s were a response to American taste, as was the phenomenon of "wall-to-wall Kerman weaving" in which rugs were actually woven by special order to fit the shapes of American rooms and hallways.

The nomadic tribal groups of Iran do to some extent preserve ancient nomadic weaving traditions in both technique and design, but the relentless march of progress is at last invading even the nomadic tent in the form of "kit" weaving. This commercial innovation represents a twentieth-century version of the cottage weaving industry of nineteenth-century Anatolia and Persia in that all raw materials for the rug are provided to the nomadic weaver as a "package," with detailed instructions, which allows the production of "Kermans" and "Kashans" in the goat-hair tents of nomadic encampments around Shiraz.

With these demurrers on the contemporary production of rugs in Persia, it should be noted, however, that thanks to strict governmental controls, and to a booming market for the finely woven Persian floor rugs using traditional designs, the technical quality of rugs being produced in many of the major weaving centers in Persia, such as Isfahan, Nayyin, Tabriz and Kashan, has reached a height probably never before attained over such a broad range of production in the entire history of rug weaving. And while the designs are modern adaptations of traditional forms, the technical virtuosity of these modern rugs, and the extraordinary degree of careful planning that has gone into their making, give them a fascination that has contributed to their extraordinarily high prices—in some cases more than a thousand dollars a square meter.

Azerbaijan, the Turkish-speaking region of northwestern Iran, is in many respects one of the country's most important weaving areas, although in terms of volume its output has never equaled that of other districts. It was the merchants of Tabriz, once the capital of Safavid Persia and now Azerbaijan's principal city, who in the latter part of the nineteenth century brought about the Persian domination of the European and American rug markets, and from this region rich in the traditions of the great Safavid dynasty, and with its proximity to Anatolia and the Caucasus, come some of the most interesting of Persian rugs.

49.
Formerly most long rugs of this type were called "camel-hair Hamadans." It is now recognized that many were made in the far northwestern area of Iran, in the Serab district, and that the light brown fiber is usually wool rather than camel hair. Like the unornamented fields of the Talish rugs woven rather close by in the Caucasus, the unornamented outer borders of Serab rugs of this type provide a kind of visual "resting place." Early twentieth century. 356 x 105 cm. (11 ft. 8 in. x 3 ft. 5 in.). George Walter Vincent Smith Art Museum, Springfield, Mass.

To the east of Tabriz, immediately south of the Soviet border, is the land of the Shah Sevan, where the weaving is in some ways virtually indistinguishable from that of the southern Caucasus. From the Serab district of this area comes a distinctive type of rug, generally long, with light brown wool used in the field and in a wide unornamented border (plate 49).

North of Tabriz, the area around the town of Heriz produces large floor rugs that show a curious mixture of Persian and Caucasian designs (plate 52). The favored design is an indented eight-lobed central medallion derived from the early sixteenth-century medallion carpets woven in this general area. But in the details these coarsely woven rugs exhibit that boldly geometric, almost "craggy" aesthetic recalling the Caucasian dragon rugs woven only a short distance to the north in former times. The oldest-known rugs from the Heriz area, woven on an all-wool foundation and dating to the nineteenth century, have been called Serabi rugs on the market, a term which lately has been used to describe any moderately old Heriz. The coarsest weavings from this area are known as Gorevan rugs, a term, like Serabi, referring more to technical quality than to a specific place of origin. The new emphasis placed by collectors on design and color, along with the fondness for geometric forms developing out of the mania for collecting Caucasian rugs, has caused the prices of Heriz carpets to go up considerably in recent times. In an attempt to capitalize on this Western taste for the geometric Caucasian forms, the production of rugs in the Meshkin area of Azerbaijan has in recent years consisted to a great extent of large and very serviceable carpets incorporating Shirvan and Kazak designs.

By contrast, the weaving around Tabriz itself has always enjoyed a high reputation, and the finest grades of modern Tabriz weaving are among the best technical products of Persian looms. In the late nineteenth century, however, Tabriz rugs were woven in a much wider variety of sizes and genres than they are at present. The enterprising merchants of Tabriz encouraged the production of finely woven silk-pile carpets which today, along with their cousins the "Heriz" silks, command ridiculously high prices (plate 50).

To the south of Azerbaijan is the Kurdistan region of Iran, in which large numbers of rugs are produced today. Perhaps in no other such small area of the rug-weaving world, with such a homogeneous population, can one find the technical variety of weaving one finds in Iranian Kurdistan. From the Hamadan district, with its bewildering subgroups named after two dozen main village collecting points, come heavily wefted, cotton-foundation, loosely woven rugs with designs borrowed from everywhere that are generally held in rather low esteem in the marketplace. Hamadan rugs do not have any recognizable design traditions, and yet some examples, especially in the larger sizes, show skillful adaptations of earlier prototypes (plate 53). In

50

certain smaller Hamadan rugs one is likely to see highly individual elements of design, demonstrating that even in this region with no distinctive traditions of design, an occasional weaver is inspired to express her own creativity in a lovely example.

In marked contrast to the technically inferior rugs of Hamadan, around the marketing center of Sehna (Sanandaj), which is the present-day capital of Kurdistan and not far from Hamadan, there were produced Turkish-knotted rugs of incredible fineness, thinness and suppleness, in which the designs almost always followed the *herati* pattern of curved leaves and palmettes. Generally woven in *sejjadeh* size or slightly larger, and very rarely if ever in what we would call a room-size format, Sehna rugs at their best, with a single-wefted construction that gives the back a curious granular texture, are among the most appealing of Persian weavings for the collector. The Sehna district seems to have been little touched by the stylistic influences of a foreign-oriented marketing structure. The geometric central medallion of most Sehna rugs, with its pendant forms at each end, was occasionally adapted to tiny formats (colorplate 1, see page 6); perhaps it is hard to think of the rug shown as only about eighty centimeters long! With its wonderful coloring and supple, tight weave, it represents village weaving of Iranian Kurdistan at its height.

Also produced in quantity in the Sehna district were flat-woven rugs that unlike the slit-tapestry-woven *kilims* of the Caucasus and Anatolia refused to compromise with the demands of the tapestry-woven technique. The larger Sehna *kilims*, about 130 x 180 cm., were often woven with the same designs as those used in Sehna pile-woven rugs (colorplate 2, see page 17), and thus from a distance it is sometimes difficult to distinguish the two techniques. So accomplished were the *kilim* weavers of this district that in some examples of their art we even see attempts at pictorial representation (plate 51).

The third major weaving center of Iranian Kurdistan is the Bijar district. Bijar rugs, known as the "iron rugs of Persia," were once woven on an all-wool foundation, but in more recent times cotton warps and wefts have been used. These rugs have an unusual construction, in which the warps are strung so closely together on the loom that, once the Turkish knotting is accomplished, they move to two levels. The back, however, appears flat since one set of warps completely obscures the other on the back of the rug. Besides the thick foundation provided by the double-warped construction, the Bijar rug has a vertical compactness produced by beating each row of knots and wool wefting after weaving with a special tool that is hit repeatedly with a heavy wooden mallet to pack the knots especially tight. The result is that Bijar rugs are so thick and stiff that it is perilous to attempt to fold one because it may simply snap in the same way that a piece of plywood would if folded. These immensely strong rugs were woven in a variety of designs, but those woven

50.
Curiously separated from the local traditions of Persian weaving, the late nineteenth-century silk carpets of Tabriz utilized designs borrowed from locations as diverse as western Anatolia and Europe. This almost rococo example shows the superb fineness of weave, subdued coloration and elaborately reflective surface characteristic of Tabriz silk rugs. Late nineteenth century. 183 x 127 cm. (6 ft. x 4 ft. 2 in.). George Walter Vincent Smith Art Museum, Springfield, Mass.

51.
Certain districts of Iran produced large numbers of rugs intended as horse trappings, and this small tapestry-woven *kilim* was evidently meant to be used as a saddle cover. The design is a three-domed *mashhad*, or holy sanctuary, and the place of weaving was the Sehna district of Iranian Kurdistan. About 1900. 85 x 96 cm. (2 ft. 9 in. x 3 ft. 2 in.). Private collection

52.
Unlike most room-sized Persian carpets, those from the district around Heriz are predominantly geometric in design, with huge, stylized forms grouped around a large central medallion. Although once looked down upon because of their comparatively coarse weave, Heriz carpets are now recognized as combining the dignity of the large Persian formats with the appeal of the geometric Caucasian designs. Early twentieth century. 722 x 498 cm. (23 ft. 9 in. x 16 ft. 4 in.). Harry Elkins Widener Memorial Room, Widener Library, Harvard University, Cambridge, Mass.

53.
While the Hamadan rugs of Iranian Kurdistan are generally of indifferent technical quality, some Hamadans woven in large formats attain visual distinction through the quality of the designs they borrow. This example, using a so-called *mina khani* (floral lattice) pattern borrowed from rugs of eastern Persia, provides a severe overall pattern that on the black ground achieves a simple elegance. Twentieth century. 549 x 355 cm. (18 ft. x 11 ft. 8 in.). Fogg Art Museum, Cambridge, Mass., gift of Mr. and Mrs. Alwin Max Pappenheimer

51

52

53

54.
The extraordinary impression made by this fine carpet from the Bijar district of Iranian Kurdistan has little to do with its enormous structural strength. Rather, it gains its effect through the placement of its simplified adaptation of a seventeenth-century arabesque design on a coal-black ground. Early nineteenth century. 823 x 457 cm. (27 x 15 ft.). Mead Art Gallery, Amherst College, Amherst, Mass.

Colorplate 19.
Not often do the large carpets woven by the settled Bakhtiari tribespeople of Iran exhibit designs that appear to form a link with their nomadic past. This exceptional example shows the application of a large-scale geometric design seemingly related to Turkoman weaving. Nineteenth century. Dimensions not given. Private collection

near the town of Garrus around 1800, with a design of huge split-leaf forms and Chinese cloud bands borrowed from classical seventeenth-century prototypes, are among the most attractive (plate 54).

South of Iranian Kurdistan is the Arak district, centered around the town of that name, formerly known as Sultanabad. From this district comes a wide variety of rugs in both commercial and traditional types; weaving in the Arak district from the late nineteenth century to about 1920 was largely under foreign control, but in more recent times it has been under the aegis of Persian entrepreneurs.

It is in the Arak district proper that those rugs known in the trade as Sarouks originate. The nineteenth-century Sarouk rug was a finely woven carpet which like the Sehna used a restricted and traditional medallion format and rarely attained room size in the Western sense. With a pendant medallion design and more curvilinear draftsmanship than Sehna rugs display, the old Sarouk exhibited a rather limited range of low-key colors together with the dark blue used as outlining for its essentially floral decoration, which in the earliest examples almost always had a somewhat angular quality (plate 55). The rugs most frequently encountered under the name Sarouk, however, are the "washed and painted" variety, marketed by the thousands in the United States, which display in their indigo and magenta palette floral forms influenced by European weaving.

To the north of the town of Arak is the broad plain of Ferahan. Older rugs of the Ferahan plain, with their characteristic *herati* designs, seem to have come to the West from the latter part of the nineteenth century onward. They are rarely encountered in an unworn condition since the wool used was evidently quite soft. Also on rare occasions one finds small rugs from the Ferahan district woven in uncharacteristic patterns that may indeed be survivors from a precommercial age. These are of such brilliance and attractiveness one wonders why more of them were not made (plate 56).

The Serabend area to the southwest of Arak produced another quite characteristic rug type, one which almost always uses a design of repeating *boteh* forms on a white or pinkish ground and is woven in a variety of sizes mainly adhering to traditional long Persian proportions (plate 57). The tendency of most Serabend rugs to follow the same pattern allowed those Westerners who so wished to furnish a house in various sizes of "matching" oriental carpets. Exceptional designs, especially those derived from seventeenth-century "compartment" rugs, were more rarely woven, and are seldom encountered in the West.

To the east of the Arak district are three urban rug-weaving centers of some importance. Kashan, which has been a major center of weaving since the sixteenth century, is today famed for the production of finely woven carpets that adhere to the design of a central medallion and four spandrels evidently invented in Persia in the

55.
The earliest Sarouk rugs from the Arak district of Iran represent rather elegant adaptations of traditional Persian designs outlined by a dark blue. This example shows the early Sarouk canon as modified, with almost humorous results, by a village weaver who had not quite mastered the design. Early twentieth century. 142 x 104 cm. (4 ft. 8 in. x 3 ft. 5 in.). George Walter Vincent Smith Art Museum, Springfield, Mass.

56.
This fragment of an unusual though severely damaged rug from the Ferahan plain in the Arak district of Iran shows a radiating medallion on a white ground. In all probability it represents the survival of a much older decorative tradition of the Arak district. Late nineteenth century. 112 x 80 cm. (3 ft. 8 in. x 2 ft. 8 in.). George Walter Vincent Smith Art Museum, Springfield, Mass.

57.
Virtually identical counterparts of this large Serabend rug, showing a design of delicate *boteh* forms on a pinkish ground, seem to have been woven in Iran by the thousands. Early twentieth century. 288 x 135 cm. (9 ft. 6 in. x 4 ft. 5 in.). George Walter Vincent Smith Art Museum, Springfield, Mass.

58.
The variation on the *herati* design found in Joshaghan rugs, where the long curved leaves are arranged in horizontal pairs, is quite distinctive and makes these Persian rugs relatively easy to identify. Early twentieth century. 254 x 168 cm. (8 ft. 4 in. x 5 ft. 6 in.). George Walter Vincent Smith Art Museum, Springfield, Mass.

55

57

56

58

latter part of the fifteenth century. Also mentioned in historical sources is the town of Joshaghan, whose modern carpet output is much smaller in volume than that of Kashan. Joshaghan rugs are again rather rarely encountered in the West; those utilizing the *herati* pattern may easily be distinguished by their clarity and angularity and the horizontal disposition of the serrated leaves (plate 58). Qumm, the third of the urban centers of this area, has been a weaving center of significance only since the second quarter of the twentieth century, and its rugs, employing techniques similar to those of Kashan rugs and, like them, occasionally including areas of silk in the pile, tend to use uniform overall patterns composed of the same classical elements found in the fields of Kashan rugs.

The Bakhtiari tribesmen and villagers, who live to the south of the Arak area, produce carpets that are distinguished in several ways. Bakhtiari weavers tend to use rather lively and bright hues instead of the restrained palette of the more commercialized carpets to the north, and their rugs are frequently woven in compartmented patterns, giving their surface the look of vividly colored tiles. At times, the settled Bakhtiari peoples have woven large carpets which seem to incorporate traditional nomadic motifs now seldom encountered in rugs of this area. A few of these older large Bakhtiari carpets, while not notable for their resistance to wear, have survived in use into our time, and present patterns of astounding force and power (colorplate 19) demanding an interior scheme which accords to the carpet a place of predominance. Many Bakhtiari carpets are woven with a fairly loosely strung warp, and have a single weft between rows of knots that is pulled very tight. As a result, on the backs of Bakhtiari rugs one often sees a speckled pattern of raised warps, a technical characteristic shared with a few weavings of the Hamadan district and with the single-wefted, but immeasurably more finely woven, rugs of the Sehna area.

In southwestern Iran lies Fars, the cradle of historical Persian civilization, which is primarily distinguished in its rug weaving by the products of non-Persian nomads such as the Khamseh (literally the "five-tribe federation") and the Qashqai (literally the "runaways"). The main marketing center for these weavings is the city of Shiraz, the capital of Fars, and indeed these tribal rugs, in which recent scholarship has distinguished the weaving of many subtribes, are generally known under the Shiraz rubric.

The rugs of the tribal weavers of Fars are of soft wool, woven loosely in brilliant colors on an all-wool foundation, with the weft frequently dyed a deep red. These distinctive nomadic rugs from Fars not only exhibit the geometric forms and sense of improvisation we see in southern Caucasian rugs but also show all sorts of characteristic ornamental techniques of their own in the selvedge and end finishes.

59.
The *sumak* technique was not confined to the Caucasus, northwestern Iran and eastern Anatolia but was extensively used in southern Iran as well. This detail from a *sumak*-brocaded rug from the Shiraz area shows the adaptability of the technique to the relatively curvilinear designs of Persian rugs. Late nineteenth century. 173 x 132 cm. (5 ft. 8 in. x 4 ft. 4 in.). Detail. George Walter Vincent Smith Art Museum, Springfield, Mass.

There is an almost endless variety of so-called Shiraz rugs, in both design and technique. One type of rug ascribed to the Qashqai is illustrative of the Shiraz genre, with its almost bewildering assortment of stylized geometric forms executed in extremely soft and lustrous wool on a coffee-colored ground (colorplate 17); these rugs frequently exhibit a multicolored selvedge, and the ends are often braided in "pigtails" or ornamented with tiny beads, cowrie shells and other *nazarlık* to ward off evil spirits.

Also produced in the nomadic milieu of southern Iran is a variety of flat-woven rugs perhaps greater than that encountered anywhere in the Islamic world, from interlocking tapestry-woven *kilims* to various kinds of brocading, including *sumak*-type weaving of almost breathtaking fineness and detail (plate 59).

Until quite recently rugs from Fars were little esteemed in Western markets, and our relative lack of knowledge of these weavings meant they did not gain the popularity which a name, and inclusion in an illustrated book, tend to confer upon a rug. Today, collectors suddenly have become aware of the variety of these rugs and of the sometimes extraordinary heights of visual expressiveness they attain as a result of their reactivity to light, clear and brilliant colors and traditional tribal designs. Partially as a response to this, the weavers north of Shiraz near Abadeh have recently begun weaving the so-called Yalameh rugs, which reproduce traditional Shiraz nomadic designs in room-size formats in much the same fashion that the Meshkin rugs of northern Azerbaijan reproduce the geometric Caucasian designs. Because of economic and social pressures, however, the actual production of the best nomadic weavings ceased in southern Iran some time ago, and today imported materials and, worse, imported coloration and aesthetics characterize a significant portion of the area's nomadic output.

To the east of Fars is the city of Kerman, which since the latter part of the nineteenth century has been perhaps the most famous of Persian rug-weaving centers. Evidently the Kerman area adapted most quickly in the last century to the production of large floor carpets for Western markets. Distinguished by a subdued color scheme which suited most furniture then in use, these Kerman rugs were fairly finely woven with a hard, long-wearing wool which bore up well under the rigors of infidel living habits. Supposedly the best Kerman rugs came from the town of Ravar to the north, and the name "Laver" Kerman, as they were mistakenly called, came to be virtually a synonym for luxurious and tasteful floor covering. Indeed, some of the early examples of this type of rug weaving, with their purplish coloration and slightly Europeanized adaptations of traditional Persian designs, exhibit visual textures and qualities of line and color that exercise an almost hypnotic effect (colorplate 18).

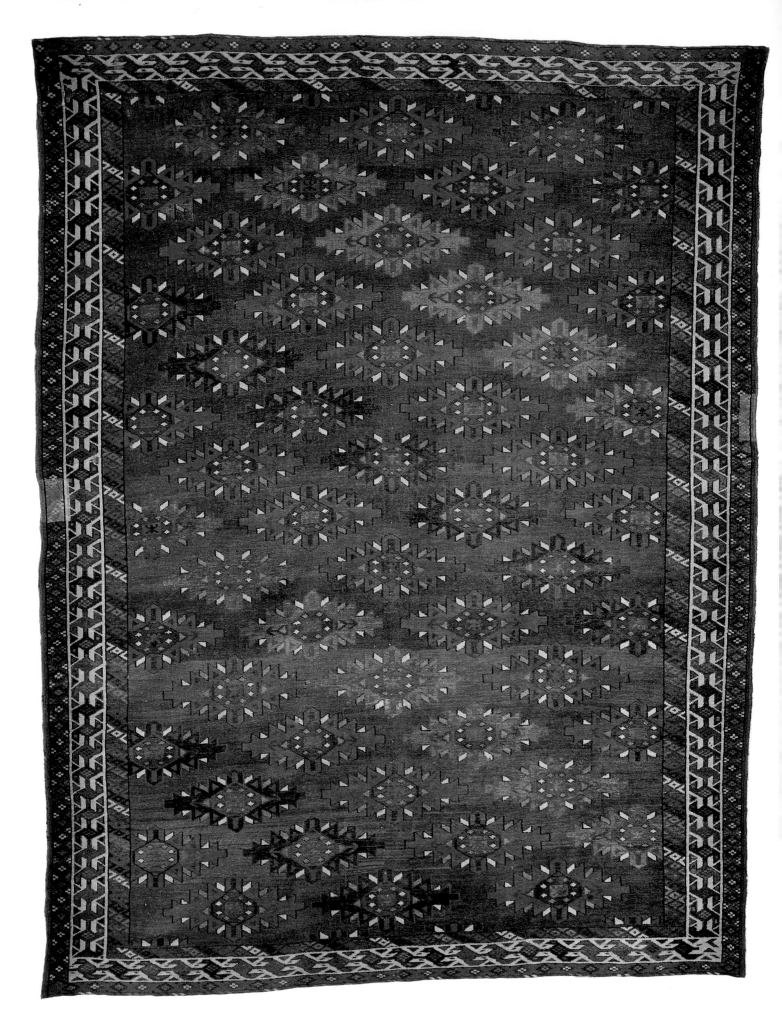

6   Turkoman Rugs

When one goes to a New England summer auction and sits under the maple trees on a sunny Saturday afternoon, one quickly becomes aware that any auctiongoer, however ignorant of rug weaving in general, can always spot a "Bukhara" carpet. Once mistakenly thought to have been woven near the Üzbek city of Bukhara, the famous "red rugs" of Central Asia, which we know today as Turkoman, or Türkmen, carpets, were and are woven by nomadic tribespeople of Turkic origin, who relied primarily upon the madder plant for the tremendous variety of red and red-brown hues that characterizes their rugs. By the late nineteenth century, these rugs, in odd, small sizes and peculiar shapes, began to find their way to the West. The small rugs, which had once been the fronts of utility bags and animal trappings, were sold cheaply, ending up in many American houses, particularly those in New England, where the majority were trampled to death underfoot. Nevertheless, a large number survived to sharpen the cutting edge of the phenomenon of rug collecting which began to burgeon in the second half of the twentieth century. In recent years Turkoman rugs have perhaps undergone closer scrutiny in print than any comparable group of rugs, with the result that some important new discoveries have been made about their history and the meaning of their forms.

The Turkoman nomads of Central Asia, who today inhabit the Türkmen Soviet Socialist Republic (Türkmenistan) and the northern parts of Iran and Afghanistan (map 5, see page 92), represent perhaps the archetypical weaving society. Our knowledge of the history of these largely illiterate and warlike peoples is gained in part through the writings of their neighbors, who frequently suffered from their raids. Of their rugs, however, we knew almost nothing until the Russian general A. A. Bogolyubov published in the early twentieth century an illustrated catalogue of the rugs he had collected while military governor of Central Asia. It is from this huge volume that

Colorplate 20.
The main carpets of the Yomud tribe, with their diagonal rows of *guls*, show a wider range of colors than the main carpets of most Turkoman tribes. This exceptional carpet is distinguished by the deep purple-red color of its ground and the lively colors of the horizontally flattened *guls*. Nineteenth century. 297 x 173 cm. (9 ft. 9 in. x 5 ft. 8 in.). Skirts not shown. Fogg Art Museum, Cambridge, Mass.

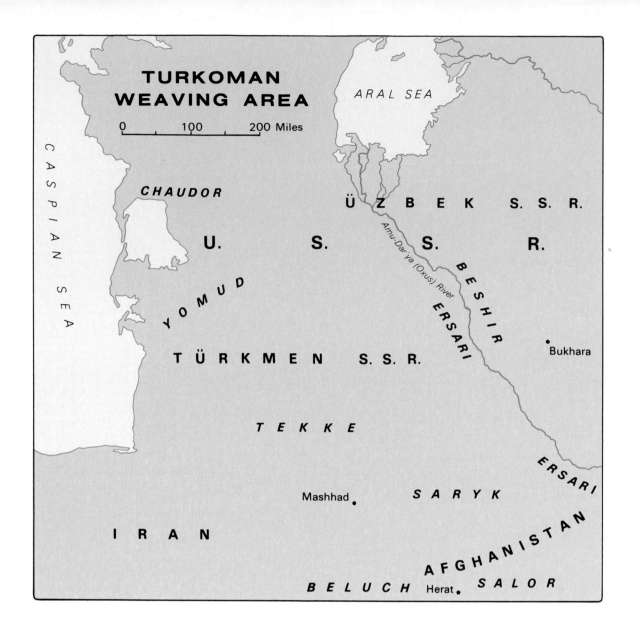

TURKOMAN
WEAVING AREA

0   100   200 Miles

CASPIAN SEA

ARAL SEA

CHAUDOR

ÜZBEK S. S. R.

U.   S.   S.   R.

Amu-Dar ya (Oxus) River

BESHIR

ERSARI

YOMUD

Bukhara

TÜRKMEN S. S. R.

TEKKE

ERSARI

Mashhad

SARYK

IRAN

AFGHANISTAN

BELUCH   Herat   SALOR

we have derived the major tribal groupings into which almost all
Turkoman rugs are categorized. There are virtually no rugs of significance produced today in Türkmenistan, and the Turkoman tribes
who live in Iran and Afghanistan, while they still weave the red rugs,
have like all nomadic peoples changed both their lifestyle and their
weaving style under the pressures of modern society.

The tribe we now call the Salor for all practical purposes ceased
to exist after its conquest by the more numerous Tekke in the nineteenth century, but as early as the tenth century the Salor, or Salghur,
were prominent in the politics of the Near East and Central Asia.
Recent research has succeeded in isolating a small group of brilliantly
colored rugs of heavy construction, with a warp on two levels,
that we now recognize as Salor weaving from before the Tekke
conquest; the British scholar Jon Thompson has dubbed this group of
early Salor rugs the "S-group." Some examples in the format of the
chuval, or tent bag (plate 61), have survived with a characteristic
repeated decoration of a medallion known in modern times as a *gul*,

a Persian word meaning flower or rose. This design, whose appearance in western Asia as early as the fifteenth century lends credence to the theory that Salor tribal groups settled in Anatolia in the aftermath of the Islamic conquest of the eleventh century, is in fact the blazon or symbol of the Salor tribe itself. There are various theories as to the origin of its palisaded octagonal shape, which may indeed in its earliest form have incorporated pictorial symbols of animals, plant forms or objects of importance in Turkoman society, such as the shortbow, arrow, tent and stirrup.

When the Salor peoples were conquered by the Tekke, their weaving appears to have undergone several transformations. Small quartered *guls* of Tekke origin, for example, were incorporated into certain types of Salor weaving, along with the Salor *guls* (colorplate 21). These weavings are quite rare, and their brilliant coloration, including an unusually lively red ground color, is often intensified by the incorporation of small amounts of madder-dyed magenta silk in the overall color scheme.

It is unlikely that the oldest extant "S-group" pieces can be positively dated much earlier than the mid-eighteenth century; and those "Salor" pieces with Tekke technique probably date to the mid-nineteenth century or later. Thus we see that of all the rug traditions we can examine, Turkoman rugs constitute at once the youngest, in terms of surviving examples, and possibly the oldest, if we accept the hypothesis, put forth by many carpet scholars, that the technique of

61.
Unlike the products woven by the later Salors under their Tekke conquerors, the older Salor rugs, the rarest and most historically important of all Turkoman rugs, show a robust technique and a design untouched by Tekke influences. This *chuval*, or tent bag, with its unflattened *guls*, is one of the earliest Salor examples known. Eighteenth century. 81 x 135 cm. (2 ft. 8 in. x 4 ft. 5 in.). Collection Arthur D. Jenkins, Mascoutah, Ill.

the pile rug entered the Islamic world through Turkoman weaving.

The Turkoman weavers wove in a wide variety of formats, but those rugs most highly valued in Turkoman tribal society were the large "main carpets" destined for floor use. The best-known Turkoman carpets are the large Tekke main carpets (plate 62), generally in a size of about 225 x 350 cm., with wide skirts of tapestry weave at each end and four or more rows of the distinctive quartered Tekke *gul*. Very rarely does one encounter an old Tekke rug of less than truly magnificent weaving quality; the pile stands up relatively straight, the wool is lustrous, ranging in hue from a brick red to a liver-colored purple in the ground. Tekke rugs of all sizes have a tendency toward the rectilinear linking of the *guls* in the field by a single or double row of dark blue knots, giving them a compartmented design if one suppresses the image of the *gul*.

The main carpets of other tribes show the *gul* form in other incarnations. The large and wide-ranging Yomud tribe to the east of the Caspian Sea used *guls* of a decidedly horizontal nature, often colored with gold yellow and a brilliant bottle green in addition to a distinctive purple red (colorplate 20). The most characteristic Yomud main carpets show these *guls* in diagonal rows of alternating colors, in contrast to the rectilinear orderliness of the Tekke rug. The Chaudor tribe employed a quite distinctive *gul* in staggered rows (plate 63); in later times the Chaudor designs appear in rugs of Yomud construction, which probably reflects, in this all-important symbolic Turkoman art, the political and cultural reality of one tribe's submission to another.

Although the smaller formats in Turkoman rugs—tent bags (*chuval*), small bags (*mafrash*), camel decorations (*asmalyk*), tent entryway hangings (*engsi*) and a myriad of other practical forms destined for specific uses in both everyday and ceremonial Turkoman life—are likely to be the most intriguing to the collector today, the finest examples of these small rugs now command prices which on a cost-per-meter basis make them among the most expensive of all rugs.

Sometimes the weaving in small pieces is quite spectacular; the fringed Chaudor *mafrash* bags (colorplate 22) occasionally show large amounts of green and a particularly lustrous pile, while the *chuval* bags of the Saryk tribe, whose weavings are particularly scarce, are much esteemed for their extraordinarily intense red-orange ground color and their fine wool (colorplate 23). More typical of Saryk bag weaving, though still hard to find, are the smaller *mafrash* bags, whose coloration tends much more toward a deep mahogany or walnut brown, with two rows of three *guls* each executed in finely woven, almost upright knotting (plate 64). By contrast, the Ersari tribal groups living along the Oxus riverbanks in the eastern part of Turkoman territory used madder dyes to produce a fire engine red in

Colorplate 21.
The Turkoman tribe known as the Salor continued to weave beautiful *chuval* bags under Tekke domination in the late nineteenth century, but the technique of such bags is closer to that of the Tekke tribe, whose tiny quartered *gul* appears in the middle of each Salor *gul*. Late nineteenth century. 74 x 112 cm. (2 ft. 5 in. x 3 ft. 8 in.). Private collection

Colorplate 22.
Few of the small Turkoman bags known as *mafrash* are as sought after by collectors as the rare Chaudor pieces. In this early example, the *guls* show a highly stylized design of two birds flanking a tree, an ancient Central Asian motif also seen in one of the earliest Anatolian rugs known, the Marby Rug (see plate 9). Early nineteenth century. 53 x 174 cm. (1 ft. 9 in. x 5 ft. 8 in.). Collection J. E. Gilbert, Thetford Center, Vt.

Colorplate 21

Colorplate 22

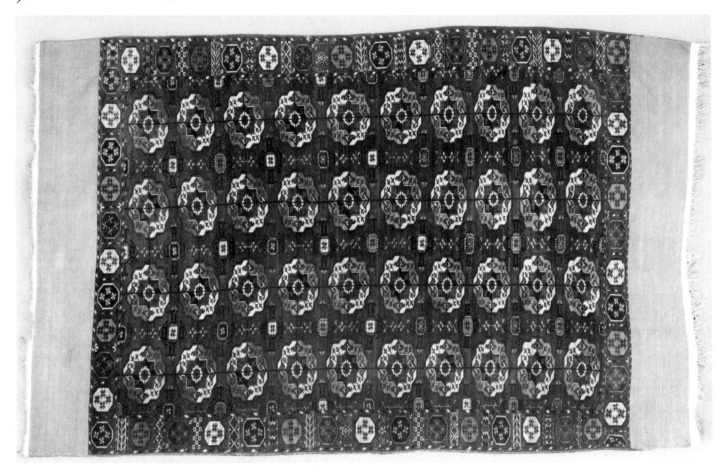

62

their *chuval* bag faces, which are among the largest of this type, often attaining a width of 160 centimeters (colorplate 24).

The rather stereotyped *chuval* bags produced by the Yomud tribe in enormous numbers demonstrate both the limitations and the variety inherent in traditional nomadic weaving. Most of these bags have nine *guls* in three rows of three within a white-ground border, and the field rarely shows any departure in design from the basic type, although the ground color ranges from the deepest purple to a bright scarlet. On the other hand, the pile-woven skirt which is found on most Yomud *chuval* bags is often decorated with unusual and variegated forms probably representing families or subgroups of the Yomud tribe (plate 66). The Ersari, who are the most widespread and diverse of all Turkoman peoples, wove *chuval* bags of many types. The Ersari along the Oxus, as we have seen, preferred a ground color of fire engine red in which the *guls*, if such they can indeed be called, seem almost melted together; in the southern part of their range, in what is today northern Afghanistan, the Ersari appear to have preferred a rich red-brown ground color, and their *chuval* bags often show forms generally thought to be more characteristic of Persian weaving (plate 65).

62.
The best known of all Turkoman rug types is the Tekke main carpet. This example, with a very dark red field and wide tapestry-woven skirts, is both typical of the genre and unusual in the richness of its color and the simplicity of its border designs. Nineteenth century. 325 x 196 cm. (10 ft. 8 in. x 6 ft. 5 in.). George Walter Vincent Smith Art Museum, Springfield, Mass.

63.
This main carpet is one of the oldest-known rugs of the Chaudor Turkomans; unlike later examples, which seem to be influenced by Yomud techniques, the early Chaudor pieces are more finely woven and exhibit a light, almost rose-red ground color. Nineteenth century. 207 x 113 cm. (6 ft. 10 in. x 3 ft. 8 in.). Textile Museum, Washington, D.C.

Another quite distinctive form of weaving among Turkoman peoples is the *engsi*, a squarish sort of rug about 165 centimeters long that was evidently intended to be hung in the doorway of the yurt, the felt-covered slat-work "tent" in which the Turkoman family lived. These rugs show a crosslike design, which has given them in the market the synthetic name of *hatchli*, meaning, literally, "with a cross." In fact, the crosslike design is probably the representation, in extremely stylized form, of a formal Islamic garden, suggesting that these hangings may have served a dual purpose, for the design may evoke that same garden of paradise which graces so many western Islamic prayer rugs. This, coupled with the pointed archlike device seen in numerous rugs of this type, indicates that the *engsi* may

63

either have been hung in the tent as a representation of the mihrab or, less likely, used on the tent floor (already covered with main carpets, if the family were wealthy) as a prayer rug.

Many Turkoman tribes wove rugs of this characteristic genre. The southwestern Tekke wove examples of particularly compact weave and lustrous wool, with a dark brown skirt of repetitive floral designs (plate 67). *Engsi* ascribed to the Yomud tribe demonstrate a much wider range of colors but a coarser weave and harsher wool; the skirts show the typical horizontal Yomud *guls*, and the selvedge is often gaily striped in red and blue (plate 68). Finally, the southern, or Afghanistan, branch of the Ersari tribe wove such rugs in its typically very coarse and robust technique, with a wide, flat selvedge in brown undyed goat hair. The color of these Ersari *engsi* is the dark mahogany red characteristic of "Afghan" rugs, into which in special examples there may intrude a bit of yellow or bottle green or sky blue in the skirt ornaments (plate 69).

The southern Ersari *engsi* rugs, among others, were frequently woven on a goat-hair warp, which, like the animal from which it comes, is quite intractable and difficult to discipline. All woolen-warped rugs of Z-spin and S-ply will tend in damp weather to curl to the front on the lower right and upper left corners and to the back on the lower left and upper right corners; those with goat-hair warps, such as the Ersari *engsi* rugs, will in damp weather do everything but get up and walk away, so reactive is this undyed goat hair to humidity changes.

Much more rare in Turkoman production is a true *sejjadeh*, or prayer rug; except for a few examples from the Tekke and Chaudor tribal groups, *sejjadeh* weaving seems to have been confined to the northern Ersari of the so-called Beshir group, who may have led a semisettled life on the farther side of the Oxus from their brethren. The *sejjadeh* rugs of the northern Ersari were woven of exceptionally soft wool, which made them extremely prone to wear. Their designs, in which the stylized arch is clearly seen, seem more closely related to the rugs of far eastern Turkestan and, ultimately, to a tradition of Chinese symbolism than to the *gul*-dominated products of the other Turkoman weavers. These exceedingly rare rugs are, despite their atypical decoration, or perhaps because of it, among the most highly prized of all Turkoman weavings (plate 70).

Perhaps the most peculiar type of Turkoman weaving, and the most uniquely adapted to the needs of Turkoman life, is the tent band (plate 72). Extending up to twenty meters in length, and from ten to sixty centimeters in width, Turkoman tent bands are much sought after by collectors, but few, if any, Western collectors have found a satisfactory way to display them since their original function was to serve as a sort of decorative frieze around the inside or the outside of the circular yurt. The end finishes of many of these extraor-

Colorplate 23.
Among the seldom-encountered weavings of the Saryk Turkomans are *chuval* bags which, like this one, are distinguished by the frequent use of cotton for whites in the pile and the very intense red orange of the lustrous wool. Nineteenth century. 88 x 122 cm. (2 ft. 11 in. x 4 ft.). Private collection

Colorplate 24.
The exceptionally large size of many of the *chuval* bags woven by the Ersari Turkomans approaches the *sejjadeh* dimensions at times, as in this so-called Beshir example from the Oxus valley. The linked decorative units on the ground of fire engine red can hardly be termed *gul* forms since they seem to have merged together with no independent existence of their own. Late nineteenth century. 96 x 160 cm. (3 ft. 2 in. x 5 ft. 3 in.). Private collection

COLORPLATE 23

COLORPLATE 24

64

65

dinary rugs are complex lattices of red, white and blue wrapped
"cables" of warp, which seem to vary from tribe to tribe. An equally
distinctive form of Turkoman weaving is the door surround, or
kapunuk, a small rug woven to form a sort of cornice around the top
of the entry of the yurt (plate 71). The practice of cabling the warps
and wrapping them in colored yarns is seen in these unusual rugs as
well.

One last example of Turkoman weaving may be cited, which shows
how broadly the term rug must be construed if it is to encompass all
the uses to which a so-called rug is put in the traditional rug-weaving
society. The *bohcha*, or bindle bag, appears to have been woven
mainly by the Yomud tribe (plate 73). On a small loom a square rug
was woven, knotted only in triangles at the four corners and plain-
woven in the center. Upon its removal from the loom, its four pile-
woven corners were folded over to the "back" of the rug and three
were sewn together, the fourth forming the envelopelike "flap" of

64.
Turkoman collectors have found that the scarcity of fine Saryk pieces is a continual problem. The highly prized Saryk *mafrash* bag faces command prices that make them perhaps the most expensive rugs in the world in terms of cost per square meter. Nineteenth century. 38 x 127 cm. (15 in. x 4 ft. 2 in.). George Walter Vincent Smith Art Museum, Springfield, Mass.

65.
A characteristic type of *chuval* bag face woven by the southern Ersari Turkomans uses a medallion form, in this example with a central octagon filled entirely with magenta silk. The meandering vine on the border of this and other southern Ersari rugs is, like the medallion, a borrowing from the Persian weaving tradition in Khurasan to the west. Early twentieth century. 53 x 169 cm. (1 ft. 9 in. x 5 ft. 6 in.). Private collection

66.
Yomud *chuval* bag faces are among the most common of all Turkoman rugs and still appear at auctions and in dealers' salesrooms with great frequency. Many examples, such as this one, however, rise above the ordinary through their unusual skirt designs. Nineteenth century. 81 x 99 cm. (2 ft. 8 in. x 3 ft. 3 in.). George Walter Vincent Smith Art Museum, Springfield, Mass.

a Turkoman variant of the modern handbag, replete with decorations of "cabled" red, white and blue wrapped ornaments.

Often grouped together with Turkoman rugs, but in fact only remotely related in style, are the rugs of the nomadic and village-dwelling Beluch people of northeastern Iran. Today most Beluch rugs are marketed through Mashhad, in Iran, or Herat, in Afghanistan, and because dealers and collectors have recently begun to explore both the primary marketplaces and the weaving centers themselves we are beginning to be able to divide Beluch rugs into quite specific weaving groups.

Beluch rugs often show a rather dark coloration, frequently with very little, if any, white in the design, and are woven in designs in imitation of Turkoman, Caucasian and Persian weaving as well as in a host of imperfectly understood Beluch tribal patterns. Many Beluch rugs are of rather shoddy construction, unappealing visually, and as a consequence the entire rug group has acquired a somewhat bad reputation. We now realize, however, that the very finest Beluch pieces, although not necessarily partaking of that aesthetic of counterpointed coloration which distinguishes the bulk of Islamic weaving, may be considered on a level with the finest in Turkoman weaving. Often the most interesting pieces are quite small in size, and many of these, using a light tawny camel brown, a considerable quantity of silk in accent areas and a surpassingly soft and silky wool, are tiny masterpieces (plate 74). Frequently encountered are Beluch prayer rugs that have a wide rectangular "arch" at the top. Beluch rugs are also noted for having quite complex end finishes with various brocaded and tapestry-woven ornaments. Beluch rugs as a group wear very poorly in floor use, which no doubt accounts for the vast numbers of sadly worn former doormats that fail to bring even an opening bid at country auctions.

66

The popularity of the Turkoman designs, with their rows of *guls* and red coloration, has led in recent times to many imitators; in addition to the wool-warped rugs still woven by Turkoman tribeswomen in northern Iran and the Soviet republic of Türkmenistan, there are commercial rugs in Turkoman designs being produced in northern Pakistan and India and, on occasion, in other parts of the rug-weaving world. These so-called Bukharas are often fine floor covering, but there is little relationship in their mechanical designs and sometimes incongruous colors to the great carpets of the tribal societies they seek to imitate.

67.
The Tekke *engsi*, or doorway hangings, are predictably among the most beautifully woven and delicately drawn of all such rugs woven by the different Turkoman tribes. The heavy, supple construction of this example is complemented by soft and lustrous wool, and the skirt designs show sprays of starlike flowers. Late nineteenth century. 157 x 124 cm. (5 ft. 2 in. x 4 ft. 1 in.). Private collection

68.
The Yomud *engsi* characteristically lacks any semblance of a prayer niche or arch, which has led some scholars to suggest that those *engsi* rugs of other Turkoman tribes that have the niche might have doubled as prayer rugs. This example shows touches of dark yellow and dark green in the skirt designs. Nineteenth century. 165 x 143 cm. (5 ft. 5 in. x 4 ft. 8 in.). Private collection

69.
This southern Ersari *engsi*, which like the *engsi* of the Yomud shows no prayer niche, has a long pile, mahogany-red ground color and a wide, flat selvedge; it also has touches of sky blue and yellow in the skirt, which add elegance and liveliness to what would otherwise be a very common design. Late nineteenth century. 173 x 124 cm. (5 ft. 8 in. x 4 ft. 1 in.). Private collection

70.
Perhaps the best known of a rare group of Turkoman *sejjadeh* rugs woven by northern Ersari tribeswomen is this famous carpet, so atypical of Turkoman weaving. The colors range from a bright yellow to a brilliant red. Nineteenth century. 167 x 103 cm. (5 ft. 6 in. x 3 ft. 5 in.). Textile Museum, Washington, D.C., bequest of Arthur J. Arwine

71

71.
The *kapunuk,* or door surround, is a form woven by several Turkoman tribes; this example is thought to be a Saryk product. Nineteenth century. Width: 110 cm. (3 ft. 7 in.). George Walter Vincent Smith Art Museum, Springfield, Mass.

72.
The design of colored pile on a warp-faced plain weave characterizes tent bands woven by all Turkoman tribes, although brocaded examples without pile ornament are also found in many tribes. Nineteenth century. Width: 28 cm. (11 in.). Detail. George Walter Vincent Smith Art Museum, Springfield, Mass.

73.
As one of the most unusual Turkoman genres, the bindle bag, or *bohcha,* has been subject to close scrutiny by scholars, who have determined that its weaving is not entirely confined to the Yomud tribe as originally thought, although most are apparently woven by the Yomuds. This example, for instance, which still bears most of its original tassel ornaments, is of Yomud weave. Nineteenth century. 74 x 69 cm. (2 ft. 5 in. x 2 ft. 3 in.). George Walter Vincent Smith Art Museum, Springfield, Mass.

72

73

74.
Good saddlebag faces are comparatively rare among the weavings of the Beluch people of eastern Iran, and those with the right combination of soft wool, dark but not dull colors and leavening in the form of bits of white pile are rarer still. The large amount of white and the liveliness of the design, with its Caucasian-like random placement of small motifs, make this example a little masterpiece. Nineteenth century. 79 x 89 cm. (2 ft. 7 in. x 2 ft. 11 in.). George Walter Vincent Smith Art Museum, Springfield, Mass.

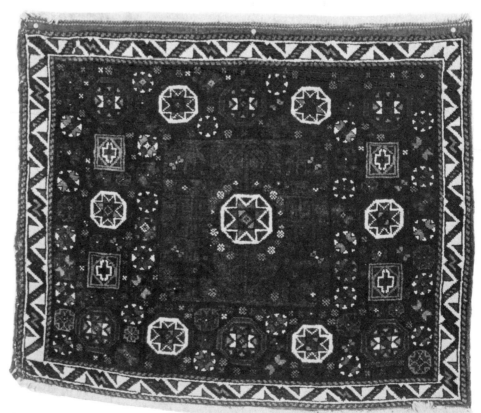

74

7 Rugs of India, East Turkestan and China

The Islamic civilization of India has to some extent always been an intruder on the subcontinent, but so lustrous were the Indian arts under the Islamic rulers of northern India and the provincial dynasties of the Deccan that they produced a unique synthesis of Islamic and non-Islamic elements which over the centuries has formed a glorious part of the artistic heritage of both civilizations. In the realm of rug weaving, however, the style of rugs woven on the subcontinent in general adheres closely to Persian models, the exceptions being those carpets woven in designs created at the court painting ateliers of the Mughal dynasty in the seventeenth and early eighteenth centuries. The use of carpets in the hot climate of India remained an anomaly, but in one case at least, that of the *sejjadeh*, the art form was established in India as a symbol of the religion of the ruling Mughal dynasty. In those periods when Islamic rulers tended to stress their orthodoxy and their control over the largely Hindu population, the religious symbolism of the prayer carpet perhaps took on greater significance.

The most spectacular of the Mughal court carpets are those which are in fact miniature paintings executed in fiber, the best-known example being a rug in the Museum of Fine Arts, Boston (colorplate 4, see page 33). The combination of fanciful elements and scenes from everyday life which characterizes Mughal art is shown in the juxtaposition of the realistic hunting scenes at the top of the composition with the imaginary beast at the bottom abducting three and a half brace of tiny black elephants while under attack by a long-feathered *simurgh*, or phoenix. The imperial Mughal taste for the bizarre is manifested in the grotesque, grinning, masklike faces filling the oval palmettes of the border, which in itself is an adaptation of those used to mount miniature paintings in the albums of wealthy Mughal patrons. The tendency of Islamic art in India toward hyperbole is

Colorplate 25.
This extraordinary Mughal prayer rug, woven in northern India, shows a breathtakingly naturalistic design of chrysanthemum blooms translated into the knotted-pile medium by the almost incredible fineness of more than 31,000 woolen asymmetrical knots per square decimeter (2000 knots per square inch). Seventeenth century. 155 x 100 cm. (5 ft. 1 in. x 3 ft. 3 in.). Private collection

75.
One of the favored forms of design in the Mughal carpets of India was the repetition on a red ground of small flowering plants, almost invariably giving the carpet a definite top and bottom for viewing. Such floral decorations can be seen in this detail from a shaped Mughal carpet designed to fit around a throne dais. Middle or second half of the seventeenth century. Length: 458 cm. (15 ft. 1 in.); varying widths. Detail of border. Museum of Fine Arts, Boston, gift of John Goelet

further seen in a Mughal prayer rug with a design of spectacularly lifelike chrysanthemums (colorplate 25).

The majority of fine Mughal rugs use a dark red, sometimes even a purple red, ground color, although a lighter rose color is also seen. In India rugs tend to be visualized in a pictorial sense in contrast to the medallion designs of Persia, which were meant to be observed from all sides. Certain shaped Mughal carpets, designed as floor revetments for particular architectural areas, exemplify the Mughal tradition of having a "top" and "bottom" (plate 75). It is possible, however, that such rugs should be considered commercial products since they are considerably coarser in weave than those rugs associated with Mughal court production.

The paradoxical combination of a taste for realism and a taste for fantasy is coupled in Indian rug weaving with the strong influence of Persian artistic traditions, which in the late sixteenth century had helped give birth to the distinctive Mughal style. Among the areas in India most receptive to the importation of Persian designs was Kashmir to the north; elaborate *sejjadeh* rugs with designs consisting of myriads of tiny flowers were probably woven in Kashmir after designs that may have originated in southern Persia in the eighteenth century at the court of the Zand dynasty in Shiraz (colorplate 26). Sometimes such rugs are so finely woven and so rigidly symmetrical that they overwhelm the viewer in a mass of detail without any overall integrity, but the truly great examples have an appeal encompassing both the courtly and the village weaving traditions in Islam. The adaptability of the weaving of northern India is almost legendary; in our own century it has produced imitations of small Kashan and Kerman *sejjadeh* rugs which only close examination will betray as Indian in origin.

The cheaper labor of India has meant that since the seventeenth century commercially produced carpets have been woven in large numbers on the subcontinent, even though for the most part their designs originated in Persia to the west. Many of the so-called Herat rugs once thought to have been produced in eastern Persia in the seventeenth century, such as those which appear draped over the tables of prosperous Dutch burghers in seventeenth- and eighteenth-century portraits (plate 24, see page 40), may have been woven in India according to designs originally from Persia. In the nineteenth and twentieth centuries, under British rule in India, the Mughal weaving traditions were continued, with prison labor in Agra being responsible for the weaving of some gigantic carpets in both Persian and Mughal designs. To the northwest, in the neighborhood of Lahore, were woven rugs of extremely fine knotting in Mughal designs (plate 76). Their density and consequent fluidity of design have not been equaled even in the commercial weaving of Nayyin or Isfahan in our own day.

Today, because of the dramatic economic changes in Iran brought about by the advent of industry financed by sales of oil, India is more and more falling heir to the Iranian weaving tradition. Large, thick Kerman-like carpets in a multitude of designs—Persian, Turkish, even Chinese-inspired creations—are being woven in India in great numbers. The finest of these may be equal to their Kerman prototypes in technical quality, but they sometimes exhibit a tendency to adapt the scale of small-format rugs to the larger room-sized carpets in demand in the West. The adaptability of Indian weavers not surprisingly causes some uneasiness in the collector of traditional handwoven carpets since this complete freeing of the weaver from indigenous design traditions may lead, and indeed has led in Persia, to carpets in imitation of photographs and even of five-dollar bills.

The technique of the pile-woven rugs, which apparently entered India in the sixteenth century with the arrival of the Mughal dynasty from Central Asia, seems also to have been foreign to China until at least the thirteenth century, when it presumably was introduced by the Mongol conquerors who would rule China for the next hundred years. In China, the age-old indigenous weaving traditions patronized by the court concentrated on those silk fabrics for which China has been justifiably famous since the dawn of recorded history. Yet the adaptation of pile-woven rugs to Chinese civilization seems to have occurred more easily than one might expect, given the enormous weight of conservative tradition in Chinese art. The reason for this was the prevalence of floor mats—that is, replaceable floor coverings of rectangular shape—already in use in the Chinese domestic milieu. We know little of the beginnings of rug weaving in China, but the established tradition of Chinese weaving seems largely to have fol-

76.
This large Lahore carpet on a rose-red ground, with its design of Mughal floral sprays arranged in a diapered pattern, is woven with more than 7700 knots per square decimeter (500 per square inch). Lahore rugs are very rarely encountered on the market, and when they are, their superior weaving quality makes them extraordinarily expensive. Late nineteenth century. 716 x 366 cm. (23 ft. 6 in. x 12 ft.). Private collection

lowed in its designs the artistic traditions in ceramics, painting and silk weaving that predated the Mongol conquest. It is possible nonetheless to discern the survival of "barbarian" Mongol designs in some of the earlier weavings still in existence.

The bulk of Chinese pile-woven rugs are fairly coarse in weave, with the exception of contemporary products of the People's Republic and of Hong Kong, which partake to some degree of the "Kerman aesthetic" of thick, plushy, tightly constructed carpets. Chinese rugs utilize a cotton warp and weft, and the wool used for the pile tends to be soft, which means the older Chinese floor rugs in general show a relatively poor resistance to wear.

Older Chinese rugs incorporating Islamic medallion-type designs are only rarely encountered. Scholars have established that certain types of overall or diapered patterns seen in Chinese rugs were adapted from the small-scale decoration of silks or little luxury objects such as porcelains and metalwork. These motifs include the geometrical repeating patterns incorporating a swastika, a Chinese symbol based on the written character whose meaning, "ten thousand," implies a wish for a long life. One of these patterns is just barely visible in the subtle field of a K'ang-hsi rug from the early eighteenth century (plate 77). The T-fret borders and the eight bunches of peonies in offset rows on the field are also characteristic Chinese motifs.

Floor rugs are only a small part of the overall rug production of China, as a wide variety of types was evolved to meet particular needs of the cultural environment. Rugs known as "pillar rugs" were designed to be wrapped around vertical columns in religious buildings; often the designs were woven so that the sewn seam formed a minimal interruption in a truly "three-dimensional" design which could be walked around and observed from all angles.

To Westerners the most powerful of Chinese symbols, and the most characteristic of Chinese art in general, is probably the dragon, which in addition to representing the cosmic universe served as a sort of blazon for the emperors who ruled China from the sixteenth into the twentieth century. The dragon traveled westward along the silk-trade routes, but its Chinese symbolism had eroded by the time it appeared in rugs of Persia and the Caucasus (plates 23 and 45, see pages 39 and 71; colorplate 12, see page 61). Together with a design of stylized waves and mountains, the dragon appears on a wide variety of Chinese rugs exported to the West, from large carpets to pillar rugs to small covers for throne cushions (plate 78).

Although never in demand in the West to the extent that the rugs of the Islamic Near East have been, Chinese rugs are beginning to be recognized as the vastly complex works of art they are. Their overall evolution is only now becoming apparent, for their intricate meanings and close relationship to the broader spectrum of Chinese art have kept them apart from much of rug scholarship until comparatively recently.

Colorplate 26.
Once believed to have been woven in southern Persia in the city of Shiraz, for the designs recall ceramic revetments of eighteenth-century buildings constructed in Shiraz under the Zand dynasty, this prayer rug with its hundreds of flowers is now thought to be from Kashmir in northern India. Eighteenth century. 173 x 107 cm. (5 ft. 8 in. x 3 ft. 6 in.). Fogg Art Museum, Cambridge, Mass., bequest of Joseph V. McMullan

Related to the Chinese carpets, and serving in fact as a sort of bridge over Central Asia between the weavings of China and those of the eastern Islamic world, are the rugs of Mongolia and, especially, the rugs of East Turkestan, which have acquired on the rug market the names of three of the area's principal cities, Samarkand, Yarkand and Khotan. The presence of sizable numbers of Muslims in the region created an artistic tradition in which the distinctions between the Islamic culture and that of China were blurred, with the two cultures sharing a common symbolism and a common aesthetic. A large carpet (plate 79) thought to be from Khotan shows a very Islamic disposition of forms with a central medallion and four spandrels, but the swastika and T-fret borders and the five dragons are of course from the Chinese artistic vocabulary. The technique of these East Turkestan rugs is another puzzle since they frequently incorporate the silk pile and metallic thread of the Polonaise carpets of seventeenth-century Iran. There is, nevertheless, a certain fascination in the mixed designs and opulent technique of these large, rather gaudy and, it must be added, impractical carpets, which may have been woven to be used in the residences of obscure Central Asian rulers, although a number have migrated westward.

Chinese weaving today occurs both inside and outside the People's Republic of China. Some of the rugs woven in the Republic represent in fact the adaptation of Kerman-type weaving of Persia, with its finely woven but very high pile, to Chinese motifs. These rugs have only recently become available in the West and are of extremely high quality. For the more traditional-minded there also exist modern reproductions of the more coarsely woven older Chinese rugs, which are often quite uncannily close to the real thing in technique, design and coloration. Other rugs woven with Chinese designs are produced in India and Hong Kong; their predominantly pastel colors and sometimes "sculptured" pile make them attractive floor covering in a limited Western market, but their place in the historical development of Chinese weaving is purely honorary.

On the rug market, Chinese rugs, until fairly recently, could as a group be considered bargains. The unstudied Chinese carpets lacking that connection between being reproduced in a book and bringing a high price in the marketplace, and the light-colored examples of some age being much thinner and more prone to wear than the "pastel Kermans," it was possible until quite a short time ago to obtain sizable Chinese carpets at auction for a fraction of the price commanded by a comparable Persian product. The overall scarcity of hand-tied knotted carpets will no doubt change this situation dramatically over the next decade, especially as the attention of scholars turns more and more to these most interesting rugs.

77.
Used to cover a *k'ang* (a heated platform found in interiors in northern China), this early eighteenth-century Chinese rug from the K'ang-hsi period (1662–1722) is decorated with peony flowers set in a diapered lattice. The colors, as in most older Chinese rugs, have paled, resulting in this case in a series of soft salmons, browns and beiges, with dark blue accents. Early eighteenth century. 117 x 81 cm. (3 ft. 10 in. x 2 ft. 8 in.). Metropolitan Museum of Art, New York, gift of William N. Cohen, 1938

78.
This Chinese throne-cushion cover shows traditional dragons surrounded by the wave-and-mountain pattern in a color scheme of reddish brown, dark blue and light yellows, blues and greens. Nineteenth century. 77 x 77 cm. (2 ft. 6 in. x 2 ft. 6 in.). Metropolitan Museum of Art, New York, bequest of Gilbert H. Montague, in memory of Amy Angell Collier Montague, 1961

79.
Large room-sized carpets reflecting such commercial dimensions of Persian rugs as nine by twelve feet were made in East Turkestan in the nineteenth century, often with traditional designs that had passed into western Asia centuries before. This large example, possibly woven in Khotan, seems to have been made for the palace of a provincial ruler, according to an inscription in Chinese that reads "Made for the palace of tranquil longevity." Late nineteenth century. 386 x 282 cm. (12 ft. 8 in. x 9 ft. 3 in.). Metropolitan Museum of Art, New York, gift of William M. Emery, 1963

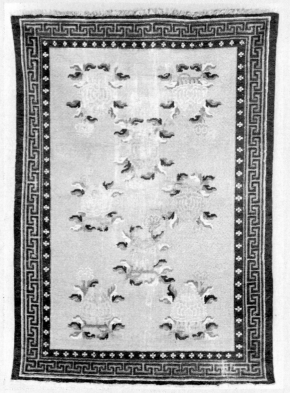

77

78

79

8 Learning About and Collecting Rugs

Thirty years ago there were relatively few serious collectors of oriental rugs as an art form, and particularly rare were collectors of the village and nomadic rugs which today are recognized as prime examples of a great folk art. To be sure, certain individuals assiduously collected rugs as a counterpoint to their interest in furniture or in an attempt to re-create period interiors, but of these only a devoted few bothered to explore the mysteries of the village and nomadic rugs. A larger number appreciated the beauty and utility of Islamic carpets as floor covering, and in certain social milieus, such as proper Boston, the oriental carpet became an integral aspect of culture; a well-educated Brahmin knew a Kerman from a Kashan at fifty yards, and oriental rugs were gathered and for the most part respected as a part of one's domestic surroundings. The suppliers of these rugs were dealers, in many cases immigrants or first-generation Westerners, who often had firsthand experience of rug weaving and dealing in their own native land. The market, as a whole, was well informed, although it invented its own attractive fictions to ensure a brisk pace of sales. The *collecting* of rugs was confined in large part to the periphery of those who *bought* rugs, but the growth of an unusual kind of literature, the Rug Book, helped to swell the ranks of serious collectors.

It is a sad fact of life that many individual species of the genus *Rug Book* fall into an ecological niche halfway between the environments of fact and fiction. Nevertheless, early in this century, a few gifted collectors and dealers began to put some order into the chaos of rug literature, a process which continues, slowly and painfully, into our own time. Gradually, with this assistance, rug collectors began to take notice of the hitherto-ignored nomadic and village rugs. The collector who came to specialize in them was able to look to the famed Ballard Collection, divided between New York and St. Louis, as an example of a balance between the revered "classical" carpets and the less venerated but often equally lovely rugs of tribe and village.

Colorplate 27.
The seventeenth-century vase carpets of central Persia produced no more attractive offspring than this brown-ground rug from the southeastern Caucasus, with its design of vegetal lattices punctuated by double-ended vase forms. As with so many Caucasian rugs, the brown knots have eroded because of the corrosive dye used, giving the carpet a sculptured effect. Nineteenth century. Approximate size: 295 x 112 cm. (9 ft. 8 in. x 3 ft. 8 in.). Detail (half). George Walter Vincent Smith Art Museum, Springfield, Mass.

Two factors are largely responsible for the tremendous surge of interest in village and nomadic rugs of the past thirty years. One is the remarkable enthusiasm of the American collector Joseph V. McMullan, which led to a number of important exhibitions and publications, and the other is the proliferation of rug societies. The serious collector may now join rug societies in New York, Toronto, London and many other places in the United States, Canada and Western Europe, and thereby may enjoy the advantages of sharing information —and misinformation—with enthusiastic colleagues and of seeing large numbers of rugs.

Naturally, the beginning collector must become familiar with the general literature on rugs; a list of well-illustrated and fairly reliable volumes is appended to this book. But the first rule a rug collector learns is to avoid excessive reliance on books and photographs. For we recognize that rugs are not only a visual but a tactile experience, and no picture can tell us about a rug's distinctive qualities as accurately as the rug itself can. Those just starting to collect rugs tend all too often to be influenced by a rug that looks like an illustration in a respected book, whereas the experienced collector is always on the lookout for the *unusual* rug that has never been reproduced anywhere—yet.

The beginning collector's entrance into the novitiate proper begins with the baptismal purchase of the first rug. There exist many ways to acquire rugs today: (1) the established rug dealer, (2) the auction, (3) the private sale or trade and (4) the miscellaneous vendor. Each has advantages and disadvantages, each has particular qualities of excitement and each offers particular opportunities for increasing one's knowledge.

The established dealer can provide the beginning collector with a great deal of practical information. The trade classifications of rugs are frequently very useful, and as more dealers interest themselves in the serious literature, they are able to provide a good combination of solid learning and that intangible personal experience which is very difficult to acquire unless one is deeply immersed in the rug business. The established dealer is frequently happy to let the collector take home a rug and try it out, and is most likely to tolerate changes of mind. His prices are more or less steady, making it possible to go somewhere else and compare rugs before buying. The large stock carried by many dealers further makes it possible to learn about different types of rugs and different qualities on the spot, and of course one may touch and stroke the merchandise, a privilege accorded by few museums.

We have already talked about rugs which have had their colors altered, either deliberately or through inadvertence, with the result that the finished product does not resemble the artifact created by the weaver. Further pitfalls await the new rug as it progresses on its career. For example, a rug may have its size altered; in past times it was quite commonplace for a rug to be narrowed or shortened, or at times even expanded, by judicious cutting and/or splicing. When buying a rug, one examines it for its overall integrity as a fabric, looking at the back for signs of cutting or joining. One examines the edges and ends; are they original or are they replaced? It is rare to find an old rug that has not undergone repairs, especially at the edges or ends, but it is best to be aware of the fact before making a purchase. The experienced collector also carefully checks a rug for evidence of dry rot, in which case dampness and bacterial action have destroyed the strength of the foundation fibers, rendering the rug largely worthless. One must look for evidence of wear that has been concealed through the application of painted dyes or the even more ubiquitous felt-tip marker pen. The telltale evidences of small or not-so-small dogs and cats may have been impossible to remove from a rug, and the rug's appearance and value are diminished as a consequence. Holding the rug up to the light is an excellent way to see holes, small or large, which may need repair. Moths may have channeled their little pathways through the pile, or worse, may have eaten the backs off the knots. Certain colors, especially the red, may have been improperly fixed, and may be prone to running, thus decreasing the monetary and aesthetic merit of the rug. The presence of certain noxious hues may have been masked by the judicious application of a solution of tea or coffee. In short, the perils to which a reasonably old rug may be subjected are almost endless.

Once one has acquired an awareness of the ways in which a rug can be "fiddled," and has developed reasonably efficacious techniques for detecting such problems, one is ready to approach the second great source of rugs, the auction. At an auction, there is no opportunity to compare prices, for the price remains ephemeral and elusive; decisive and informed action is essential. Few reputable dealers will sell a "fiddled" rug without pointing out its faults, but in an auction the maxim is *caveat emptor*, and the buyer must be wary indeed. There are two general principles for auction buying, known to every experienced collector. First, one must never bid on a rug one has not had the opportunity to examine carefully beforehand. Second, one must set a limit on one's bidding beforehand, and adhere to it. All collectors agree on these principles, and in every major rug auction collectors may be seen violating them, especially the second.

In many auctions, the private collector will quickly notice a group of muttering, whispering individuals standing to one side of the hall. This is an ad hoc organization known as "the ring" or "the coalition." It is a group consisting of dealers and "pickers" (independent individuals who make a living selling to dealers) who have agreed not to bid against each other. They will buy as many rugs as they can, and later will have their own little auction, known as a "knockout," where some members of the coalition will receive rugs and others will receive money. While the ring is not legal in many states, it is an accepted fact of life at some auctions. Generally, the presence of a ring means that there will be no great bargains at that particular sale.

Buying from private individuals, or from such miscellaneous vendors as antiques dealers, combines some of the reassuring aspects of buying from an established dealer with the excitement of bargain hunting in an auction. In every case, the prudent collector will ask for a receipt identifying the rug and specifying the price paid, and will undertake reasonable inquiries to make sure the rug being purchased actually belongs to the seller. In an age when prices of rugs are increasing astronomically as the supply shrinks and the number of serious, even fanatical, collectors grows, the theft of rugs is becoming more and more ordinary, and the serious collector keeps an inventory of rugs, together with photographs of each rug, in a safe place along with an itemized "fine arts" insurance policy.

Having acquired a small collection, the collector is then faced with a new set of problems. How should rugs be displayed? How should they be cleaned? How should they be repaired?

To display rugs, one must first weigh whether the rug should be used on the floor, or hung, or placed on an article of furniture. If the decision is to hang, many dealers will explain how to sew a piece of cotton or jute tape to the top of the rug, through which a metal or wooden rod can be placed to enable the rug to be hung.

Cleaning rugs should follow two basic principles. First, the rug should be physically rubbed, scrubbed, wrung and squeezed as little as possible. Second, all residue of whatever soap or mild detergent has been used should be carefully removed. Good commercial cleaning with forced-jet water and neutral detergent is often one of the best ways to clean a rug, but the rug should be carefully tested for strength and colorfastness before cleaning. Likewise, edges and ends prone to unravel should be overcast before washing, as a rug may otherwise lose length and/or width through washing.

The repair of rugs raises both practical and ethical questions. The best repairers today can perform miracles so marvelous that their work cannot be detected by any but the most sharp-eyed experts. This raises the question of whether—and to what extent—one should repair an old work of art such as a rug at the risk of substantially reconstituting, and even reinterpreting, its visual assets. For most collectors, this problem seldom arises, for the repairing of a rug today is such an expensive undertaking that few can afford to indulge in extensive reweaving and renapping. By contrast, the vital repairs to edges and ends are relatively inexpensive; many dealers will teach the collector how to make these simple repairs, and some will even show one how to renap and reweave as well. Before having repair work done, one should be sure to get a written estimate; one may wish to mark those spots to be repaired with bits of brightly colored yarn.

The effect of repairs on the value of a rug depends on many things, among them the obtrusiveness and age of the repair. Many old rugs have repairs, and a beautifully repaired old rug should not be thought of with any less charity than one would accord an old painting with a few repainted areas or an antique automobile with a reconstituted fender—given all the horrible things that can happen to rugs, one must be amazed that repairs are found as infrequently as they are; they are an inevitable part of collecting, and the experienced collector learns to recognize them for what they are.

In addition to frequenting places where rugs are sold, the collector usually seeks the company of others sharing the same collecting mania. Such company will be found at the rug societies, which also provide collectors with many opportunities for learning. These include programs with guest speakers, exposure to the collections (and egos) of other collectors, special information on publications and field trips to museum collections.

Museum collections (a list of some of the more noteworthy ones is appended) are indeed another important place for a serious collector and student of rugs to learn. Here, however, those habits acquired in the salesroom and auction hall, where one pokes, prods and pulls at rugs, must be rigorously suppressed. For museums, rugs are both a joy and a problem. The wave of interest in village and nomadic rugs, for instance, means that exhibitions of them, many of which have been held over the past three decades, are astonishingly well attended, a fact which has turned the heads even of those museums which were formerly the most disdainful of them. But rugs take a very large amount of space to display, and as a result few museums are able to show more than a very small number at one time. Museum curators are often harassed by individuals wanting to see rugs, a process which means much rolling and unrolling for the curator. The experienced collector recognizes the practical limitations placed upon a museum, and usually manages to see rugs in storage areas by arranging for a special group visit through a rug society, whereby the curator's labors are performed for the benefit of the maximum number of aficionados.

The formal study of rugs is, despite all the broad public interest, an undertaking in which very few individuals are able to participate. A few museums sponsor series of lectures or smaller and more intimate seminars where interested individuals may hear qualified experts discuss various aspects of the history, technique and aesthetics of rugs. The formal study of carpets as an element of regular university course work, however, hardly exists. Still, rug study has advanced tremendously in the past fifteen years, through publications and symposia connected with exhibitions, through on-site research in many rug-weaving areas by qualified scholars, and through the phenomenon of collecting, which has brought to scholarly attention many examples of rugs which might otherwise have been worn out and forgotten.

In a few decades, the handweaving of rugs as a viable commercial enterprise and as an integral part of traditional society will be a memory. But the revolution in attitude toward rugs in our own time, which has led us to regard deserving examples as works of art rather than simply as utilitarian objects to be used up and thrown out, gives us some hope that future generations will be able to enjoy these sensual, tactile, visual masterpieces for their designs, colors and textures and for the insights they offer into a way of life where the creation of beauty with one's own hands was a vital part of existence.

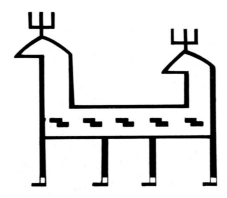

Glossary

abrash, unintentional variations in color on a rug caused by irregular dyeing; generally appears as horizontal stripes (see colorplate 9).

brocading, a technique used in weaving flat-woven rugs, in which supplementary (extra) wefts, which form the design of the rug, wholly or partially cover the basic warp and weft. The *sumak* technique (figure 4) is one form of brocading.

chuval (juval, tschowal), a large bag, generally wider than it is deep, used for clothing and other personal belongings, and hung as decoration inside the Turkoman tent.

engsi, sometimes called *hatchli* ("with a cross"), a type of rug that served instead of a door at the entrance to the Turkoman tent, and may have been used for prayer as well.

gul (gol, gül), the medallionlike design motif characteristic of particular Turkoman tribal groups, which is generally octagon-shaped and appears in repeating rows on Turkoman rugs.

heddle, a part of a loom; a wooden stick attached to the lower warps by loops of string, used to pull the lower warps through and above the upper warps (figure 2).

heybe (khorjin), the small double saddlebags found in all parts of the Islamic rug-weaving world, generally woven continuously in one piece and often cut up into two decorated bag faces.

kilim (gileem), a weft-faced tapestry-woven rug of the so-called slit variety, in which slits appear in the fabric where two colors meet in a vertical line (figure 3). The term is used also as another name for the slit-tapestry technique itself.

knot, the basic structural unit of the pile rug; knots vary according to local and tribal weaving traditions, with the two main types being the symmetrical (Turkish, Gördes) and asymmetrical (Persian, Sehna) varieties (figure 5).

mafrash, a small bag woven by Turkoman nomads, generally much wider than it is deep, used to hold small articles of clothing and other personal belongings. The term is also used for a variety of bag forms in Iran and Turkey.

mihrab, a recess or niche in the wall of a Muslim house of prayer which faces the Holy City of Mecca; often depicted in a more or less architectural form in *sejjadeh* rugs.

sejjadeh, an Arabic term denoting a rug suitable for prayer, approximately 100 x 155 cm. in dimensions; often applied to any rug of that size but more commonly to one bearing in its design a depiction, however abbreviated, of the mihrab.

selvedge, the edge of a rug on the long side; its technical construction may vary widely from area to area and from period to period, thus forming an important technical identifying characteristic of a rug.

shed stick, a part of a loom; a wooden stick, or slat, used to separate alternate warps on a loom into upper and lower groups (figure 2). See *heddle*.

skirt, an area at one or both ends of a rug which is separate in design, and at times in technique, from the field of the rug and its borders. Turkoman rugs are well known for their wide, tapestry-woven skirts.

sumak, a form of weft-wrapping or brocading, used in many flat-woven rugs (figure 4). The term is also applied to a rug woven in the *sumak* technique.

warp, the longitudinal strands forming the foundation of the rug; the warps constitute the basic element of all woven fabrics when woven together with the wefts, including both flat-woven and knotted rugs (figure 2).

weft, strands which form the latitudinal part of a rug's foundation when woven into the warps on a loom.

yastık, a term employed in Turkey for small rugs woven approximately twice as long as wide, intended for the faces of cushions but used for many other purposes as well.

Reading and Reference

General Works on the History of Carpets

DIMAND, M. S., AND JEAN MAILEY. *Oriental Rugs in the Metropolitan Museum of Art.* New York: Metropolitan Museum of Art, 1973.

ERDMANN, KURT. *Oriental Carpets.* Translated by Charles Grant Ellis. 2d ed. New York: Universe Books, 1962.

ERDMANN, KURT. *Seven Hundred Years of Oriental Carpets.* Translated by May H. Beattie and Hildegard Herzog. Berkeley and Los Angeles: University of California Press, 1970.

A Manual of Contemporary Collectable Rugs

EILAND, M. L. *Oriental Rugs.* Rev. and exp. ed. Boston: New York Graphic Society, 1976.

Works with a Technical Orientation

TATTERSALL, C. E. C. *Notes on Carpet-Knotting and Weaving.* London: Victoria and Albert Museum, 1969.

THOMPSON, JON. *The Anatomy of a Carpet.* Parts 1–3. Published as appendixes to a series of auction catalogues. London: Lefevre & Partners, 1977.

Works on Particular Groups of Rugs

AZADI, SIAWOSCH. *Turkoman Carpets.* Translated by Robert Pinner. Fishguard, Wales: Crosby, 1975.

BIDDER, HANS. *Carpets from Eastern Turkestan.* Translated by Grace Marjory Allen. New York: Universe Books, 1964.

ELLIS, CHARLES GRANT. *Early Caucasian Rugs.* Washington, D.C.: Textile Museum, 1975.

ERDMANN, KURT. *The History of the Early Turkish Carpet.* Translated by Robert Pinner. London: Oguz Press, 1977.

ETTINGHAUSEN, RICHARD; M. S. DIMAND; LOUISE W. MACKIE; AND CHARLES GRANT ELLIS. *Prayer Rugs.* Washington, D.C.: Textile Museum, 1974.

MACKIE, LOUISE W. *The Splendor of Turkish Weaving.* Washington, D.C.: Textile Museum, 1973.

SCHÜRMANN, ULRICH. *Caucasian Rugs.* London: Allen and Unwin, 1967.

YETKIN, SERARE. *Early Caucasian Carpets in Turkey.* London: Oguz Press, 1978.

Some Useful and Well-Illustrated Catalogues

BACHARACH, JERE L., AND IRENE A. BIERMAN. *The Warp and Weft of Islam.* Seattle: Henry Art Gallery, University of Washington, 1978.

LANDREAU, ANTHONY N., ed. *Yörük: The Nomadic Weaving Tradition of the Near East.* Pittsburgh: Museum of Art, Carnegie Institute, 1978.

LANDREAU, ANTHONY N., AND W. R. PICKERING. *From the Bosporus to Samarkand: Flat-Woven Rugs.* Washington, D.C.: Textile Museum, 1969.

McMULLAN, JOSEPH V. *Islamic Carpets.* New York: Near Eastern Art Research Center, 1965.

McMULLAN, JOSEPH V., AND DONALD O. REICHERT. *The George Walter Vincent and Belle Townsley Smith Collection of Islamic Rugs.* Springfield, Mass.: George Walter Vincent Smith Art Museum, 1970.

TSCHEBULL, R. *Kazak.* New York: Near Eastern Art Research Center and New York Rug Society, 1971.

New and Noteworthy

HALI: *The International Journal of Oriental Carpets and Textiles.* London: Oguz Press, 1978.

Some Public Collections of Oriental Rugs

UNITED STATES

Boston: Museum of Fine Arts
Cambridge, Mass.: Fogg Art Museum, Harvard University
Cincinnati: Cincinnati Art Museum
New York City: The Metropolitan Museum of Art
Philadelphia: Philadelphia Museum of Art
St. Louis: The St. Louis Art Museum
Springfield, Mass.: George Walter Vincent Smith Art Museum
Washington, D.C.: The Textile Museum

OTHER

Amsterdam: Rijksmuseum
Athens: Benaki Museum
Berlin, East: Islamisches Museum
Berlin, West: Museum für Islamische Kunst
Budapest: Iparmüvészeti Múzeum (Museum of Applied Arts)
Florence: Museo Bardini e Galleria Corsi
İstanbul: Türk ve İslam Eserleri Müzesi (Museum of Turkish and Islamic Art)
Vakıflar Müzesi (Museum of Pious Foundations)
Lisbon: Museu Calouste Gulbenkian
London: Victoria and Albert Museum
Lyons: Musée Historique des Tissus
Milan: Museo Poldi Pezzoli
Paris: Musée des Arts Décoratifs
Tehran: The Carpet Museum of Iran
Vienna: Österreichisches Museum für angewandte Kunst

Index

Acknowledgments

Cooper-Hewitt staff members have been responsible for the following contributions to the series: concept, Lisa Taylor; administration, John Dobkin and Christian Rohlfing; coordination, Pamela Theodoredis. In addition, valuable help has been provided by S. Dillon Ripley, Joseph Bonsignore, Susan Hamilton and Robert W. Mason of the Smithsonian Institution, as well as by the late Warren Lynch, Gloria Norris and Edward E. Fitzgerald of Book-of-the-Month Club, Inc.

The author would like to express his special thanks to Brenda Gilchrist, Lisa Little, Joseph Bourke Del Valle and Joan Hoffman for their patience, tenacity and good sense in dealing with a difficult manuscript and its illustrations. The manuscript was improved by suggestions from three specialists, Milton Sonday, Sarah Sherrill and Daniel Walker, for which the author is indeed grateful. To Charles Grant Ellis, Thomas Chatalbash, David Stansbury, Jack Irvine and a host of friends and colleagues too numerous to mention, or too shy to want to be mentioned, go thanks beyond expression. These friends and colleagues having helped above and beyond the call of duty, it remains to add that the book's shortcomings may be credited entirely to the author.

Credits

Allen Memorial Art Museum, Oberlin College, Oberlin, Ohio: Color 13. Antikvarisk-topografiska Arkivet, Stockholm: 9. Bildarchiv Preussischer Kulturbesitz, West Berlin: Color 3. John Denny: 1. Erkin Emiroğlu: 8. Fogg Art Museum, Harvard University, Cambridge, Mass.: 14, 53, 60, 61; gift of Elizabeth Gowing, Harborne W. Stuart, Peggy Coolidge and the Estate of W. I. Stuart in memory of Mr. and Mrs. Willoughby H. Stuart, Jr.: 29, 44, 46 and color 6, 11, 17, 20 by Michael A. Nedzweski and Barry Donahue. George Walter Vincent Smith Art Museum, Springfield, Mass.: 35, 36, 39, 40, 49, 50, 55–58, 62, 64, 66, 71–74; color 16. Color 1, 2, 9, 27 by David Stansbury. Tony Landreau: 2–5. The Metropolitan Museum of Art, New York: 13, 15, 16, 20, 21, 30, 77–79; color 14 (Otto E. Nelson). Muldoon Studio: Color 8. Musée Historique des Tissus, Lyons: 17. Museum of Fine Arts, Boston: 32, 75; color 4, 5. Trustees of the National Gallery, London: 12. National Gallery of Art, Washington, D.C.: 25. Otto E. Nelson: Color 26. Novosti Press Agency (A.P.N.): 6, 7. Österreichisches Museum für angewandte Kunst, Vienna: 18, 19, 45. William W. Owens, Jr.: Color 19. Yanni Petsopoulos: 33. Private collections, courtesy of the owners: 43; color 18, 21, 25. Rijksmuseum, Amsterdam: 24, 27. The St. Louis Art Museum: 28. David Stansbury: 31, 34, 41, 42, 47, 48, 51, 52, 54, 59, 65, 67–69, 76; color frontispiece, 7, 10, 15, 22–24. The Textile Museum, Washington, D.C.: 10, 11, 23, 63, 70; color 12. Topkapı Palace Museum, Istanbul: 26. Richard Wagner: 37, 38. William Rockhill Nelson Gallery of Art, Kansas City, Mo.: 22.

MAPS: Jean Paul Tremblay
LINE DRAWINGS: Fran Gazze Nimeck
ORNAMENTS: Richard Schindler